# THE MUSHROOM GROWER'S HANDBOOK

"Unlock the Secrets of Mycology with Step-by-Step Instructions, Tips, and Troubleshooting for Novice and Experienced Growers"

BY

James Wylie

# TABLE OF CONTENT

# CHAPTER 3

## GROWING MUSHROOMS: STEP BY STEP



# CHAPTER 4:

## ADVANCED TECHNIQUES AND TROUBLESHOOTING



# CONCLUSION



# APPENDIX:

# INTRODUCTION

Welcome to the enchanting world of mushroom cultivation! Whether you're a curious novice eager to embark on a fascinating journey or an experienced grower seeking to enhance your skills, "The Mushroom Grower's Handbook" is your comprehensive guide to unlocking the secrets of successful mushroom cultivation.

In this handbook, we delve into the captivating life cycle of mushrooms, from the mystical spore to the bountiful harvest. You'll discover the joy of growing your own mushrooms, not only for the delectable flavors they bring to your table but also for the therapeutic and sustainable aspects of cultivating these incredible fungi.

We begin our exploration by introducing you to the diverse and magical realm of mushrooms, shedding light on the numerous benefits of cultivating your own. From there, we guide you through the essential steps of getting started, helping you choose the right species and assemble the necessary tools for your mushroom-growing venture.

As you progress through the chapters, you'll gain a deep understanding of the mushroom life cycle, substrate selection, and the fundamental techniques that form the backbone of successful cultivation. Detailed step-by-step instructions will empower you to navigate the journey from inoculation to harvest with confidence, while insights into advanced techniques and troubleshooting tips will equip you for any challenges that may arise.

Whether you're cultivating mushrooms for personal enjoyment or considering a larger-scale commercial operation, "The Mushroom Grower's Handbook" is your trusted companion. Join us as we explore the mysteries of mycology and celebrate the joy of harvesting your own homegrown mushrooms.

Get ready to embark on a rewarding adventure, where the magic of fungi comes to life in your own home or garden. Happy growing!

# The Fascinating World of Mushrooms

## Understanding the Magic of Fungi

Understanding the magic of fungi encompasses a multifaceted exploration into the captivating world of these often-misunderstood organisms. Let's break down a comprehensive explanation of this fascinating realm:

**Understanding the Magic of Fungi**

The term "fungi" encapsulates an incredibly diverse kingdom of organisms, ranging from the familiar mushrooms that grace our plates to the microscopic mycelium weaving through soil and wood. At its core, understanding the magic of fungi involves grasping several key concepts:

**1. Ancient Dance of Fungi and Humanity**

Fungi have entwined with human history since ancient times. They've been revered for their mystical qualities in folklore, medicine, and cultural practices across various civilizations. From the spiritual significance attributed to mushrooms by indigenous cultures to the use of fungal compounds in traditional medicine, their influence on human societies is profound.

**2. Mycelium: Nature's Network**

Mycelium, the intricate web of fungal threads, serves as the foundation of the fungal kingdom. Beneath the surface, mycelium creates vast networks, acting as nature's ultimate recyclers and symbiotic partners to plants. Its ability to decompose organic matter and form symbiotic relationships with trees, known as mycorrhizae, contributes significantly to ecosystems' health and resilience.

### 3.Benefits of Growing Your Own Mushrooms

Cultivating mushrooms at home goes beyond a simple gardening endeavor. It embodies a connection to nature, a deeper understanding of ecosystems, and a way to embrace sustainability. Beyond these aspects, the act of nurturing and harvesting your own mushrooms offers therapeutic benefits, promoting mindfulness and a sense of accomplishment.

### 4. Medicinal Properties and Health Benefits

Mushrooms are renowned for their medicinal properties, containing compounds that exhibit antioxidant, anti-inflammatory, and immune-boosting effects. From the beta-glucans found in many species that support immune function to specific compounds in certain mushrooms linked to potential anti-cancer properties, exploring the medicinal potential of fungi is a burgeoning field of research.

### 5. Environmental Applications and Mycoremediation

Fungi possess an incredible ability to break down and detoxify pollutants in the environment, a process known as mycoremediation. Their role in bioremediation—cleaning up contaminants like oil spills or pesticides—showcases their potential in restoring ecosystems and mitigating environmental damage.

### 6. Culinary Delights

Finally, the culinary world embraces mushrooms for their diverse flavors and textures. From the umami-rich notes of Shiitake to the delicate crunch of Enoki, mushrooms offer a palette of tastes to elevate culinary creations, making them an integral part of gastronomy across cultures.

Understanding the magic of fungi encompasses their historical significance, ecological roles, health benefits, and culinary allure, painting a comprehensive picture of their multifaceted contributions to our world.

# Benefits of Growing Your Own Mushrooms

Cultivating mushrooms at home extends beyond the joy of a rewarding hobby; it brings forth an array of benefits that touch upon various aspects of well-being and sustainability. In this section, we delve into the numerous advantages of embarking on the journey of growing your own mushrooms.

**From Garden to Table: The Joy of Homegrown Harvests**

1. Nurturing a Connection to Nature

Growing your own mushrooms fosters a deep and tangible connection to the natural world. Witnessing the miraculous transformation from spore to harvest instills a sense of appreciation for the intricate processes of life. Engage in the therapeutic practice of nurturing these fascinating organisms, promoting mindfulness and a heightened awareness of the cycles of nature.

2. Freshness Beyond Compare

Harvesting mushrooms directly from your cultivation space ensures unparalleled freshness. Unlike store-bought varieties that may have traveled long distances, homegrown mushrooms offer a flavor and texture that captivates the palate. Elevate your culinary experiences with a bounty that is not only delicious but also harvested at the peak of its nutritional value.

**Cultivating Connection: The Therapeutic Aspects of Mushroom Growing**

1 Stress Reduction and Mindful Cultivation

The act of cultivating mushrooms can serve as a therapeutic and stress-relieving endeavor. Engaging in the mindful practices of tending to your mycelial companions and observing the incremental growth stages fosters a sense of calm and connection. The rhythmic nature of mushroom cultivation provides an opportunity to escape the hustle of daily life and find solace in the simplicity of nurturing life.

2. Educational Opportunities and Skill Development

Growing mushrooms at home presents a continuous learning experience. From understanding the intricacies of mycology to mastering the art of maintaining optimal growing conditions, each step offers valuable insights. Sharpen your observational skills, develop a deeper understanding of ecosystems, and cultivate a unique expertise that extends beyond the realm of mushroom cultivation.

**Sustainable Living and Environmental Impact**

1 Reducing Carbon Footprint

Home mushroom cultivation aligns with sustainable living practices. By producing your own mushrooms, you contribute to the reduction of the carbon footprint associated with commercial agriculture and transportation. The localized nature of home cultivation minimizes the environmental impact, fostering a more eco- conscious lifestyle.

*2 Waste Reduction through Mycoremediation.*

Mushrooms possess the remarkable ability to break down and remediate various types of organic matter. Harness this mycoremediation potential to repurpose agricultural waste or unused substrates, contributing to waste reduction efforts. Transforming organic waste into nutrient-rich compost further underscores the sustainability of mushroom cultivation.

**Cost-Efficiency and Accessibility**

*1 Economical Home Gardening*

Growing your own mushrooms can be a cost-effective alternative to purchasing them. With minimal equipment and resources, you can establish a home cultivation setup, providing a sustainable source of high-quality mushrooms at a fraction of the cost of store-bought equivalents.

*2 Access to Rare and Specialty Varieties*

Home cultivation opens doors to a vast array of mushroom varieties, including rare and specialty species that may be challenging to find commercially. Explore the diversity of flavors, textures, and medicinal properties that these unique mushrooms offer, enriching your culinary and wellness experiences.

Embarking on the journey of growing your own mushrooms not only yields a bountiful harvest but also nurtures a connection to nature, promotes well-being, contributes to sustainability, and enhances your culinary repertoire. The benefits extend far beyond the physical act of cultivation, enriching various facets of life in a truly holistic manner.

# CHAPTER 1

# GETTING STARTED

## Choosing the Right Mushroom Species

*Understanding Popular Varieties for Home Cultivation*

Choosing the right mushroom species for home cultivation is a pivotal decision that sets the stage for a rewarding and successful venture into mycology. In this section, we delve into the distinctive attributes of some popular varieties, exploring their growth requirements and the culinary delights they bring to the table.

### The Versatility of White Button Mushrooms

*1 Characteristics and Growth Preferences*

White Button mushrooms, scientifically known as *Agaricus bisporus*, are a versatile and adaptable choice for beginners. These mushrooms thrive in a substrate rich in organic matter, such as compost, and exhibit rapid mycelial colonization. Understanding their preference for cooler temperatures during fruiting is key to optimizing growth conditions.

*2 Culinary Uses and Popular Recipes*

Known for their mild flavor, White Buttons serve as a culinary staple. From salads to soups, their versatility in the kitchen makes them an excellent choice for those new to mushroom cultivation. Embracing White Buttons not only provides a reliable harvest but opens the door to a wide array of culinary possibilities.

## Exploring the Rich Flavors of Shiitake Mushrooms

*1 Growing Conditions for Shiitake*

Shiitake (*Lentinula edodes*) introduces cultivators to a more complex flavor profile. Understanding their preference for hardwood logs as a substrate and the nuanced environmental conditions required for successful cultivation reveals the intricacies of growing Shiitake.

*2 Enhancing Your Culinary Repertoire with Shiitake*

In the kitchen, Shiitake's robust and savory taste adds depth to various dishes. Stir-fries, soups, and traditional Asian cuisine benefit from the unique flavor that Shiitake brings. Choosing Shiitake not only broadens one's mycological expertise but also elevates the culinary experience.

## Oyster Mushrooms: A Colorful and Nutritious Option

*1 Understanding Oyster Mushroom Growth*

Oyster mushrooms (*Pleurotus spp.*) captivate growers with their vibrant colors and rapid growth. They thrive on a variety of substrates, showcasing adaptability. Exploring their mycelial growth and optimal fruiting conditions unveils the potential for visually stunning and nutritionally rich harvests.

*2 Cooking Tips and Culinary Delights*

Beyond their aesthetic appeal, Oyster mushrooms contribute a delicate flavor to dishes. From vegetarian stir-fries to pizza toppings, understanding Oyster mushrooms' culinary attributes adds a dynamic dimension to the home grower's kitchen.

## Beyond the Ordinary: Enoki and Maitake Mushrooms

*.1 Unique Characteristics and Growing Techniques*

Enoki (*Flammulina velutipes*) and Maitake (*Grifola frondosa*) offer unique growth patterns and flavors. Enoki requires cooler temperatures and increased air exchange, while Maitake demands specific substrate selection and ample space for its elaborate frond-like structure to develop.

*.2 Adding Enoki and Maitake to Your Culinary Palette*

In the kitchen, Enoki's delicate texture complements salads and Asian-inspired dishes, while Maitake's robust flavor enhances various culinary creations. Cultivators embracing these varieties diversify their mushroom repertoire and elevate their culinary experiences.

Choosing the right mushroom species involves a thoughtful consideration of preferences, skill level, and desired culinary outcomes. Each variety brings its own charm, challenges, and unique flavors, providing cultivators with a rich tapestry of options to explore in the world of home cultivation.

# Popular Varieties for Home Cultivation
*1: Exploring Diverse Mushroom Options*

Choosing the right mushroom varieties for home cultivation is an exciting step that opens the door to a diverse and flavorful world. In this section, we'll introduce you to some popular and accessible varieties, providing insights into their unique characteristics and cultivation preferences.

**White Button Mushrooms (*Agaricus bisporus*)**

*.1 Characteristics and Growth Preferences*

White Button mushrooms, with their mild flavor and versatile nature, are an excellent choice for beginners. Explore the characteristics of their mycelium, rapid colonization, and their preference for a substrate rich in organic matter. Understanding these nuances is key to creating an optimal environment for White Button cultivation.

*.2 Culinary Uses and Popular Recipes*

Delve into the culinary world of White Button mushrooms. From enhancing salads to starring in creamy soups, learn about the versatile applications of this classic variety. Discover popular recipes that showcase the simplicity and delightful taste of homegrown White Buttons.

## Shiitake Mushrooms (*Lentinula edodes*)

*1 Growing Conditions for Shiitake*

Shiitake mushrooms, known for their robust flavor, require specific conditions for successful cultivation. Understand the role of hardwood logs in their growth, and explore the nuanced environmental parameters that contribute to a thriving Shiitake harvest.

*.2 Culinary Repertoire Enhancement*

Discover the culinary richness that Shiitake brings to the table. From stir-fries to traditional Asian dishes, Shiitake's savory notes elevate a variety of recipes. Uncover the art of incorporating homegrown Shiitake into your culinary repertoire.

## Oyster Mushrooms (*Pleurotus spp.*)

*.1 Understanding Oyster Mushroom Growth*

Oyster mushrooms, celebrated for their vibrant colors and rapid growth, thrive on a variety of substrates. Explore the adaptability of Oyster mushrooms and gain insights into the intricacies of their mycelial growth and optimal fruiting conditions.

*.2 Culinary Tips and Delights*

Beyond their visual appeal, Oyster mushrooms contribute a delicate and unique flavor to dishes. Learn culinary tips for incorporating Oyster mushrooms into vegetarian stir-fries, pasta dishes, or even as a flavorful pizza topping.

**Enoki and Maitake Mushrooms**

*Unique Characteristics and Growing Techniques*

Explore the distinctive qualities of Enoki (*Flammulina velutipes*) and Maitake (*Grifola frondosa*). From Enoki's slender stems to Maitake's frond-like structure, understand the unique characteristics and cultivation techniques for these special varieties.

*Culinary Palette Expansion*

Diversify your culinary experiences with Enoki and Maitake. Discover the delicate texture of Enoki in salads and Asian-inspired dishes, and explore Maitake's robust flavor in sautés and hearty soups. Embrace the opportunity to add these unique mushrooms to your culinary palette.

Choosing popular varieties for home cultivation provides a delightful entry into the world of mushroom growing. Whether you're drawn to the classic appeal of White Button mushrooms or the unique characteristics of Enoki and Maitake, each variety offers a rewarding and flavorful experience for home cultivators.

# Matching Mushrooms to Your Growing Environment

Cultivating the Perfect Habitat

Selecting the right mushroom species is essential, but creating an environment tailored to their unique needs is equally critical. This section guides you through the process of harmonizing your growing space with the specific requirements of your chosen mushrooms.

**Microclimates and Temperature Control**

*1* Understanding Microclimates

Different mushrooms thrive in distinct microclimates. Recognizing and creating these microclimates involve understanding temperature variations, humidity levels, and light exposure. This section provides insights into identifying the microclimates that suit your chosen mushrooms, ensuring optimal growth conditions.

2 Temperature Control Strategies

Temperature plays a pivotal role in mushroom cultivation. Learn effective strategies for maintaining the right temperature range within your growing environment. Whether utilizing climate-controlled chambers, heating mats, or natural insulation, mastering temperature control is crucial for cultivating healthy and productive mushrooms.

**Humidity and Moisture Management**

*Embracing the Humidity Needs of Mushrooms*

Mushrooms thrive in high humidity environments, but the specific requirements vary among species. Explore methods for maintaining the ideal humidity levels, including misting systems, humidity chambers, and natural approaches. This section provides practical tips for preventing substrate drying or over-saturation.

*Moisture Retention Techniques*

Understanding the moisture needs of different mushrooms is paramount. Tailor your substrate and employ moisture-retention techniques to match the preferences of your selected varieties. Techniques such as casing layers and precise watering schedules are explored, ensuring the optimal moisture content for successful cultivation.

## Light and Air Exchange Considerations

*Balancing Light Exposure*

While mushrooms don't require light for growth, they respond to light cycles for fruiting initiation. Gain insights into managing light exposure through natural and artificial sources, ensuring your mushrooms receive the right cues for the fruiting phase.

*Ensuring Adequate Air Exchange*

Healthy mycelial growth and successful fruiting demand a consistent exchange of fresh air. Discover techniques for achieving optimal air exchange within your growing space. Learn the importance of fresh air, the regulation of carbon dioxide, and methods for preventing contaminants through proper ventilation.

## Substrate Specifics: Tailoring the Growth Medium

*Substrate Composition for Different Varieties*

Crafting the ideal growth medium is essential for successful mushroom cultivation. Delve into the specifics of substrate composition, considering the unique requirements of your chosen mushrooms. Explore the use of various organic materials and understand the role of nitrogen content for maximum yield and quality.

*Importance of Sterilization and Pasteurization*

Maintaining a sterile growing environment is crucial. This section details methods for substrate sterilization and pasteurization, ensuring a clean slate for your mushrooms to thrive. Learn when each technique is most appropriate to safeguard your growing medium against contaminants.

Matching mushrooms to your growing environment involves a nuanced understanding of their microclimate preferences, temperature control, humidity management, light exposure, air exchange needs, and substrate customization. By fine-tuning these elements, you create an environment where your chosen mushrooms can flourish, ensuring a successful and fulfilling cultivation experience.

# Essential Tools and Equipment

**Essential Tools and Equipment for Successful Mushroom Cultivation**

*Section 3.1: Building Your Mycological Toolkit*

As you embark on the journey of mushroom cultivation, having the right tools and equipment is crucial for creating a conducive and efficient environment for your fungi to thrive. In this section, we'll explore the essential items needed to set up your mycological toolkit.

## Pressure Cooker or Autoclave

*Sterilization Precision*

A pressure cooker or autoclave is a cornerstone of mushroom cultivation. It ensures the sterilization of substrates and equipment, preventing contamination from competing microorganisms. Learn about the proper use and maintenance of these devices to guarantee a sterile growing environment for your mushrooms.

## Substrate Jars or Bags

*Crafting the Ideal Growing Medium*

Substrate jars or bags provide a controlled environment for the growth of mycelium. Understand the types of substrates suitable for different mushroom varieties and how to prepare them in jars or bags. This section guides you through the substrate preparation process, emphasizing the importance of proper sterilization.

## Inoculation Tools

*Precision and Aseptic Technique*

Inoculation tools, such as syringes or inoculation loops, are essential for introducing mushroom spores or mycelium into the substrate. Mastering aseptic technique during inoculation is crucial to prevent contamination. Explore the different inoculation methods and the proper handling of these tools to ensure successful colonization.

## Fruiting Chamber or Growing Environment

*Creating the Ideal Conditions*

A dedicated fruiting chamber or growing environment is essential for the transition from mycelium to mushroom fruiting. Learn how to design and maintain a space that provides the right conditions for humidity, fresh air exchange, and proper lighting. This section outlines the key considerations for constructing an effective fruiting chamber.

## Hygrometer and Thermometer

*Monitoring Environmental Parameters*

A hygrometer and thermometer are indispensable for keeping track of humidity and temperature levels within your growing environment. Gain insights into how these tools assist in maintaining optimal conditions for mycelial growth and fruiting.

## Spray Bottle or Misting System

*Fine-Tuned Humidity Control*

Maintaining proper humidity is critical for successful mushroom cultivation. Discover the role of a spray bottle or misting system in achieving finely tuned humidity levels, especially during the fruiting stage. Learn when and how to apply moisture without risking over-saturation.

**Scalpel or Knife for Harvesting**

*Precision Harvesting Techniques*

Harvesting your mushrooms requires precision to avoid damage to the mycelium and future flushes. Explore the use of a scalpel or knife for clean and careful harvesting. This section provides tips on the best practices for harvesting your homegrown mushrooms.

**Cleaning Supplies**

*Maintaining a Sterile Environment*

Maintaining cleanliness throughout the cultivation process is vital. Learn about the cleaning supplies needed to sanitize your workspace, tools, and equipment. Understand the importance of a sterile environment in preventing contamination and ensuring the success of your mushroom cultivation endeavors.

Equipping yourself with the right tools and equipment is a foundational step towards successful mushroom cultivation. This section guides you through the essential items necessary for a sterile, controlled, and efficient mycological toolkit, setting the stage for a bountiful harvest

# Creating a Functional Mushroom Workspace

*Designing an Efficient Cultivation Environment*

Establishing a dedicated and well-organized workspace is essential for successful mushroom cultivation. In this section, we'll explore the key elements and considerations for creating a functional mushroom workspace.

## Location and Lighting

*Selecting an Appropriate Space*

Choose a location that provides stability in terms of temperature and avoids direct sunlight. Consider the accessibility of power sources for lighting and equipment. This section offers insights into selecting an ideal space for your mushroom cultivation endeavors.

*Lighting Considerations*

While mushrooms don't require light for growth, adequate lighting is essential for tasks such as maintenance, harvesting, and monitoring. Explore options for ambient lighting or portable sources to ensure a well-lit workspace.

## Work Surfaces and Sterile Zones

*Designing Sterile and Non-Sterile Zones*

Define distinct areas within your workspace for sterile and non-sterile activities. Learn how to set up work surfaces, such as laminar flow hoods or glove boxes, to maintain aseptic conditions during critical stages like inoculation and substrate preparation.

## Storage Solutions

*Organizing Substrates, Tools, and Equipment*

Efficient storage is vital for maintaining an organized workspace. Explore storage solutions for substrates, tools, and equipment. Learn how to label and categorize items to streamline the cultivation process.

## Ventilation and Air Exchange

*Ensuring Fresh Air Flow*

Proper ventilation is crucial to prevent the buildup of contaminants. Understand how to implement a ventilation system that ensures consistent fresh air exchange in your workspace. This section provides insights into creating an environment conducive to healthy mycelial growth.

## Temperature and Humidity Control

*Fine-Tuning the Cultivation Environment*

Maintaining optimal temperature and humidity levels is key to successful mushroom cultivation. Explore methods for temperature control, such as insulation or heating, and learn how to fine-tune humidity levels using misting systems or humidifiers.

## Organization and Workflow

*Streamlining Cultivation Processes*

Developing an efficient workflow is essential for managing tasks throughout the cultivation cycle. Explore organizational strategies and workflow designs to streamline activities from substrate preparation to harvesting. This section provides insights into creating a systematic and effective cultivation process.

## Safety Measures and Hygiene Protocols

*Prioritizing Safety and Hygiene*

Implementing safety measures and hygiene protocols is paramount. Learn about essential safety gear, such as gloves and masks, and establish hygiene practices to minimize the risk of contamination. This section emphasizes the importance of a clean and safe workspace.

**Record Keeping and Monitoring**

*Tracking Progress and Adjusting Conditions*

Maintaining detailed records of your cultivation processes is essential for troubleshooting and improvement. Explore record-keeping techniques and monitoring systems to track environmental conditions, growth patterns, and harvest yields.

Creating a functional mushroom workspace involves thoughtful planning and organization. By implementing the principles outlined in this section, you'll design an environment that promotes efficiency, cleanliness, and optimal conditions for successful mushroom cultivation.

# Must-Have Tools for Successful Mushroom Cultivation

Building Your Essential Toolkit

A well-equipped toolkit is essential for successful mushroom cultivation. In this section, we'll explore the must-have tools that will empower you throughout the various stages of the cultivation process.

**Pressure Cooker or Autoclave**

*Sterilization Precision*

A pressure cooker or autoclave is indispensable for ensuring the sterilization of substrates and equipment. This tool is essential for preventing contamination and creating a sterile environment conducive to healthy mycelial growth.

## Substrate Jars or Bags

*Crafting the Ideal Growing Medium*

Substrate jars or bags are containers for preparing and holding the growing medium. They play a crucial role in creating a controlled environment for mycelial colonization. Understanding the types of substrates suitable for different mushroom varieties is key to successful cultivation.

## Inoculation Tools

*Precision and Aseptic Technique*

Inoculation tools, such as syringes or inoculation loops, are vital for introducing mushroom spores or mycelium into the substrate. Mastering aseptic technique during inoculation is crucial to prevent contamination and ensure successful colonization.

## Fruiting Chamber or Growing Environment

*Creating the Ideal Conditions*

A dedicated fruiting chamber or growing environment is essential for transitioning from mycelium to mushroom fruiting. Learn how to design and maintain a space that provides the right conditions for humidity, fresh air exchange, and proper lighting.

## Hygrometer and Thermometer

*Monitoring Environmental Parameters*

A hygrometer and thermometer are indispensable for keeping track of humidity and temperature levels within your growing environment. These tools assist in maintaining optimal conditions for mycelial growth and fruiting.

## Spray Bottle or Misting System

*Fine-Tuned Humidity Control*

Maintaining proper humidity is critical for successful mushroom cultivation. A spray bottle or misting system enables you to achieve finely tuned humidity levels, especially during the fruiting stage, without risking over-saturation.

## Scalpel or Knife for Harvesting

*Precision Harvesting Techniques*

A scalpel or knife is essential for clean and careful harvesting of your mushrooms. Precision during the harvesting process avoids damage to the mycelium and supports future flushes.

## Cleaning Supplies

*Maintaining a Sterile Environment*

Cleaning supplies are crucial for maintaining a sterile environment throughout the cultivation process. Learn about the necessary items to sanitize your workspace, tools, and equipment, ensuring a contamination-free cultivation space.

## Work Surfaces and Sterile Zones

*Designing Sterile and Non-Sterile Zones*

Define distinct areas within your workspace for sterile and non-sterile activities. Implement work surfaces such as laminar flow hoods or glove boxes to maintain aseptic conditions during critical stages like inoculation and substrate preparation.

## Storage Solutions

*Organizing Substrates, Tools, and Equipment*

Efficient storage is vital for maintaining an organized workspace. Explore storage solutions for substrates, tools, and equipment. Label and categorize items to streamline the cultivation process.

## Ventilation and Air Exchange

*Ensuring Fresh Air Flow*

Proper ventilation is crucial to prevent the buildup of contaminants. Explore methods for implementing a ventilation system that ensures consistent fresh air exchange in your workspace.

Equipping yourself with these must-have tools ensures that you are well-prepared to navigate the various stages of mushroom cultivation, from substrate preparation to harvesting. Having a comprehensive and functional toolkit is a key factor in the success of your cultivation endeavors.

Understanding the Mushroom Life Cycle

*From Spore to Harvest - Navigating the Mushroom Life Cycle*

A fundamental understanding of the mushroom life cycle is crucial for successful cultivation. In this section, we'll explore the various stages that mushrooms go through, from the humble spore to the bountiful harvest.

# Chapter 2

# The Basics of Mushroom Cultivation

## Understanding the Mushroom Life Cycle

*From Spore to Harvest - Navigating the Mushroom Life Cycle*

A fundamental understanding of the mushroom life cycle is crucial for successful cultivation. In this section, we'll explore the various stages that mushrooms go through, from the humble spore to the bountiful harvest.

## Germination

*Spore The Beginning of Life*

The mushroom life cycle begins with spore germination. Explore the conditions and factors that initiate spore germination, leading to the development of mycelium. Understand the importance of a sterile environment during this critical stage.

## Mycelial Growth

*The Mycelium Network*

As spores germinate, they give rise to mycelium, a network of fine, thread-like structures. Delve into the intricacies of mycelial growth, exploring how it colonizes the substrate and establishes the foundation for future mushroom development.

## Substrate Colonization

*Mycelium's Takeover*

During substrate colonization, mycelium expands and engulfs the growing medium. Learn about the visual cues and milestones that indicate successful colonization. Understand the importance of maintaining optimal environmental conditions for robust mycelial growth.

## Primordia Formation

*Precursors to Mushrooms*

Primordia are small, pin-like structures that signify the imminent arrival of mushrooms. Explore the environmental triggers and conditions necessary for the initiation of primordia formation. Understand how the mycelium transitions from colonization to the preparation for fruiting.

## Fruiting Initiation

*Setting the Stage for Mushrooms*

Fruiting initiation marks the transition from mycelial growth to the development of mature mushrooms. Explore the factors that trigger fruiting, including light exposure, temperature changes, and humidity adjustments. Understand the role of the primordia in the upcoming mushroom harvest.

## Mushroom Development and Maturation

*The Culmination of Efforts*

Witness the maturation of mushrooms from small, undeveloped structures to fully formed caps and stems. Understand the visual indicators of maturity and the optimal timing for harvesting to ensure the best flavor, texture, and nutritional content.

## Spore Release and Reproduction

*Completing the Cycle*

Spore release is the final stage of the mushroom life cycle, completing the reproductive cycle. Explore how mature mushrooms release spores into the environment, contributing to the potential for new mycelial growth and the initiation of subsequent life cycles.

## Resting Phase and Environmental Signals

*Preparing for the Next Cycle*

After spore release, mushrooms enter a resting phase. Explore how environmental signals, such as changes in temperature and humidity, influence the onset of the next life cycle. Understanding the resting phase is crucial for planning and managing subsequent cultivation cycles.

A comprehensive understanding of the mushroom life cycle provides cultivators with the knowledge needed to navigate each stage successfully. From spore germination to spore release, each phase contributes to the fascinating journey of mushroom cultivation.

# Understanding the Mushroom Life Cycle

*From Spore to Harvest - Navigating the Mushroom Life Cycle*

A fundamental understanding of the mushroom life cycle is crucial for successful cultivation. In this section, we'll explore the various stages that mushrooms go through, from the humble spore to the bountiful harvest.

**Spore Germination**

*The Beginning of Life*

The mushroom life cycle begins with spore germination. Explore the conditions and factors that initiate spore germination, leading to the development of mycelium. Understand the importance of a sterile environment during this critical stage.

**Mycelial Growth**

*The Mycelium Network*

As spores germinate, they give rise to mycelium, a network of fine, thread-like structures. Delve into the intricacies of mycelial growth, exploring how it colonizes the substrate and establishes the foundation for future mushroom development.

## Substrate Colonization

*Mycelium's Takeover*

During substrate colonization, mycelium expands and engulfs the growing medium. Learn about the visual cues and milestones that indicate successful colonization. Understand the importance of maintaining optimal environmental conditions for robust mycelial growth.

## Primordia Formation

*Precursors to Mushrooms*

Primordia are small, pin-like structures that signify the imminent arrival of mushrooms. Explore the environmental triggers and conditions necessary for the initiation of primordia formation. Understand how the mycelium transitions from colonization to the preparation for fruiting.

## Fruiting Initiation

*Setting the Stage for Mushrooms*

Fruiting initiation marks the transition from mycelial growth to the development of mature mushrooms. Explore the factors that trigger fruiting, including light exposure, temperature changes, and humidity adjustments. Understand the role of the primordia in the upcoming mushroom harvest.

## Mushroom Development and Maturation

*The Culmination of Efforts*

Witness the maturation of mushrooms from small, undeveloped structures to fully formed caps and stems. Understand the visual indicators of maturity and the optimal timing for harvesting to ensure the best flavor, texture, and nutritional content.

**Spore Release and Reproduction**

*Completing the Cycle*

Spore release is the final stage of the mushroom life cycle, completing the reproductive cycle. Explore how mature mushrooms release spores into the environment, contributing to the potential for new mycelial growth and the initiation of subsequent life cycles.

**Resting Phase and Environmental Signals**

*Preparing for the Next Cycle*

After spore release, mushrooms enter a resting phase. Explore how environmental signals, such as changes in temperature and humidity, influence the onset of the next life cycle. Understanding the resting phase is crucial for planning and managing subsequent cultivation cycles.

A comprehensive understanding of the mushroom life cycle provides cultivators with the knowledge needed to navigate each stage successfully. From spore germination to spore release, each phase contributes to the fascinating journey of mushroom cultivation.

# From Spore to Mycelium: A Journey Through Growth Stages

*The Genesis of Mycelial Expansion*

Embarking on the journey from spore to mycelium is a captivating process that forms the foundation for successful mushroom cultivation. In this section, we'll delve into the intricate stages that mark the growth of mycelium, paving the way for the flourishing mushroom life cycle.

## Spore Germination: Initiating Life

*Unveiling the Potential*

The journey begins with spore germination, a remarkable process where dormant spores awaken to life. Explore the factors and conditions that trigger spore germination, unlocking the genetic potential encapsulated within these microscopic entities.

## Hyphal Exploration: The Birth of Mycelium

*The Emergence of Hyphae*

As spores germinate, they give rise to delicate thread-like structures known as hyphae. Journey through the mesmerizing landscape of hyphal exploration, where these strands extend, intertwine, and form the intricate network that defines mycelium.

## Mycelial Growth: Colonizing the Substrate

*The Expansion Unleashed*

With hyphae in full force, mycelial growth takes center stage. Witness the colonization of the substrate as mycelium spreads its delicate network, breaking down organic matter and establishing the groundwork for the eventual emergence of mushrooms.

## Maturing Mycelium: Preparing for Fruiting

*The Transition to Maturity*

As mycelium matures, it undergoes structural changes in preparation for the fruiting stage. Explore the visual cues that indicate maturing mycelium and the pivotal role it plays in setting the stage for the development of primordia.

## Fruiting Initiation: A Prelude to Mushrooms

*The Unveiling of Primordia*

Fruiting initiation marks a transformative phase where primordia, the tiny pin-like structures, emerge. Delve into the environmental triggers and conditions that prompt this initiation, signaling the imminent arrival of the mushroom fruiting stage.

## Fungal Symphony: Orchestrating Mushroom Growth

*Crafting Mushroom Structures*

As the primordia develop, witness the intricate process of mushroom growth and maturation. Explore how environmental factors and internal mechanisms orchestrate the formation of mushroom caps, stems, and gills, culminating in the fully realized, edible fungi.

## Spore Release: Completing the Cycle

*Sowing the Seeds for the Future*

The culmination of the mushroom life cycle occurs with spore release. Explore how mature mushrooms release countless spores into the environment, seeding the potential for new mycelial growth and perpetuating the fascinating cycle from spore to mycelium once more.

Embarking on the journey from spore to mycelium unveils the intricate dance of life within the fungal kingdom. Each stage brings forth its unique wonders, laying the groundwork for the flourishing growth of mushrooms in the cyclical narrative of cultivation.

# Key Factors Influencing Mushroom Development

The Dance of Environmental Variables

Mushroom development is a nuanced process influenced by various environmental factors. In this section, we'll explore the key elements that play a crucial role in shaping the growth, maturation, and overall development of mushrooms.

**Temperature Dynamics**

*Balancing Warmth and Coolness*

Temperature serves as a master orchestrator in mushroom development. Explore the optimal temperature ranges for different mushroom varieties, understanding how fluctuations influence mycelial growth, primordia formation, and the overall maturation process.

**Humidity Harmony**

*The Art of Moisture Management*

Maintaining the right humidity levels is paramount for successful mushroom development. Delve into the delicate balance between moisture and air, discovering how humidity influences mycelial growth, primordia formation, and the prevention of issues such as drying or over-saturation.

**Light Cycles and Photoperiod**

*Illuminating the Fruiting Stage*

While mushrooms don't require light for growth, light cycles play a crucial role in signaling the onset of the fruiting stage. Explore the impact of light exposure on primordia initiation and maturation, and understand how manipulating photoperiods can optimize mushroom development.

## Fresh Air Exchange

*Breathing Life into the Environment*

A consistent exchange of fresh air is vital for healthy mushroom development. Investigate the importance of ventilation in preventing the buildup of carbon dioxide and ensuring optimal oxygen levels. Learn how proper air exchange contributes to robust mycelial growth and successful fruiting.

## Substrate Composition and Nutrition

*Crafting a Nutrient-Rich Habitat*

The substrate composition forms the foundation for mushroom nutrition. Explore the role of various organic materials in providing essential nutrients for mycelial growth and mushroom development. Understand the nuances of substrate composition for different mushroom varieties.

## Carbon Dioxide Regulation

*Managing the Gaseous Environment*

Carbon dioxide ($CO_2$) levels influence mushroom development, and regulating its concentration is crucial. Explore techniques for managing $CO_2$ levels within the growing environment, ensuring that mushrooms receive the right cues for optimal growth and fruiting.

## Microclimate Considerations

*Tailoring Conditions for Specific Mushrooms*

Understanding microclimates is key to matching mushrooms to their ideal growing conditions. Delve into the microclimate preferences of different varieties, including temperature, humidity, and air exchange. Learn how to create customized environments to support the unique needs of specific mushrooms.

## Nutrient Timing and Supplementation

*Enhancing Growth with Strategic Nutrition*

Timing and supplementation of nutrients can significantly impact mushroom development. Explore strategies for nutrient supplementation during key growth stages, ensuring that mushrooms have access to the nutrients needed for robust mycelial growth and bountiful fruiting.

A nuanced understanding of these key factors influencing mushroom development empowers cultivators to fine-tune their cultivation environments. By skillfully navigating the interplay of temperature, humidity, light, air exchange, substrate nutrition, and other variables, cultivators can optimize conditions for the successful growth and maturation of their mushrooms.

# Substrate Selection and Preparation

*Crafting the Foundation for Mycelial Prosperity*

Substrate selection and preparation are pivotal steps in mushroom cultivation, influencing the quality and yield of your harvest. In this section, we'll delve into the art and science of choosing the right substrate and preparing it to create an optimal environment for mycelial growth.

## Understanding Substrate Basics

*Unveiling the Role of Substrates*

Substrates serve as the nourishing foundation for mycelial growth. Explore the fundamental principles of substrate selection, understanding the role of organic materials in providing essential nutrients for mushrooms. Delve into the considerations for choosing substrates suitable for different mushroom varieties.

## Common Substrate Materials

*Exploring Organic Ingredients*

Dive into the world of common substrate materials used in mushroom cultivation. From grains and straw to sawdust and wood chips, understand the unique characteristics of each material and their suitability for specific mushroom species. Explore the nuances of combining different substrates for a well-rounded nutritional mix.

## Substrate Preparation Techniques

*Mastering Sterilization and Pasteurization*

Achieving a clean and sterile substrate is paramount for successful mycelial growth. Explore substrate preparation techniques, including sterilization and pasteurization methods. Understand when to use each technique based on the substrate materials and the specific requirements of your chosen mushrooms.

## DIY Substrate Recipes

*Crafting Nutrient-Rich Blends*

Unlock the art of creating your own substrate recipes tailored to the needs of your mushrooms. Explore DIY formulations using readily available ingredients. Learn about nutrient-rich blends that promote vigorous mycelial growth and set the stage for a prolific fruiting phase.

## Adjusting pH Levels

*Balancing Acidity for Optimal Growth*

pH levels play a crucial role in mycelial growth, and adjusting acidity is essential for cultivating certain mushroom varieties. Delve into the importance of pH monitoring and learn techniques for modifying pH levels to create an environment conducive to robust mycelial colonization.

## Moisture Content and Watering Techniques

*Nurturing the Right Amount of Moisture*

Balancing moisture content is a delicate art in substrate preparation. Explore the significance of maintaining the right level of hydration for mycelial growth. Learn about effective watering techniques, including misting and hydration schedules, to ensure optimal substrate conditions.

## Sterile Techniques for Substrate Inoculation

*Ensuring a Clean Start*

The inoculation of substrates is a critical step in the cultivation process, demanding sterile techniques to prevent contamination. Explore best practices for maintaining aseptic conditions during substrate inoculation, using tools such as laminar flow hoods or glove boxes.

**Troubleshooting Substrate Issues**

*Addressing Challenges for Mycelial Success*

Troubleshoot common substrate issues that may arise during the cultivation journey. From contamination concerns to substrate dryness, gain insights into identifying and resolving challenges to ensure a healthy and flourishing mycelial environment.

Mastering substrate selection and preparation is an art that requires a nuanced understanding of mushroom requirements and careful attention to detail. By navigating the considerations outlined in this section, cultivators can create a nutrient-rich, sterile, and optimal substrate environment, setting the stage for a successful mushroom cultivation endeavor.

# Choosing the Right Substrate for Your Mushrooms

The Art of Substrate Selection

Selecting the right substrate is a crucial decision in the mushroom cultivation journey, influencing the growth, yield, and overall success of your harvest. In this section, we'll explore the considerations and factors involved in choosing the optimal substrate for your specific mushroom species.

**Understanding Mushroom Preferences**

Tailoring Substrates to Mushroom Varieties

Different mushrooms have distinct preferences when it comes to their growing medium. Explore the specific substrate requirements for popular mushroom varieties, understanding the unique nutritional needs and environmental conditions that foster their optimal development.

**Common Substrate Materials**
Diverse Ingredients, Diverse Options

Delve into the world of common substrate materials used in mushroom cultivation. From grains and sawdust to straw and wood chips, understand the characteristics of each material and its suitability for various mushroom species. Explore the versatility of combining multiple substrates to create nutrient-rich blends.

**Matching Substrates to Mushroom Characteristics**
Aligning Substrate Features with Mushroom Traits

Consider the inherent characteristics of your chosen mushrooms when selecting a substrate. Explore how factors such as mycelial colonization speed, substrate colonization preferences, and fruiting conditions influence the choice of substrate. Learn to match substrate features with the unique traits of your mushrooms.

**DIY Substrate Formulations**
Crafting Customized Growing Mediums

Unlock the art of creating DIY substrate formulations tailored to your mushrooms' needs. Explore recipes using readily available ingredients, incorporating elements like grains, sawdust, and additional nutrients. Learn how to customize substrate blends to enhance mycelial growth and encourage abundant fruiting.

**Considering Environmental Conditions**

Harmonizing Substrates with Growing Environments

Environmental factors play a pivotal role in substrate performance. Explore how temperature, humidity, and air exchange in your cultivation space impact the effectiveness of different substrates. Understand the importance of aligning substrate choices with the specific conditions of your growing environment.

**Availability and Cost Factors**

Balancing Accessibility and Budget
Consider the practical aspects of substrate selection, taking into account the availability and cost of materials. Explore economical options that meet the requirements of your mushrooms while considering the sustainability and accessibility of substrate materials.

**Compatibility with Cultivation Methods**

Aligning Substrates with Cultivation Techniques
Different cultivation methods may require specific substrate characteristics. Explore how substrate choices align with methods

such as agar-to-grain transfers, liquid inoculations, or monotubs. Understand how substrate compatibility contributes to the success of your chosen cultivation approach.

**Evaluating Past Success and Learning Experiences**

Drawing Insights from Cultivation History
Reflect on past cultivation experiences to gather insights into substrate performance. Evaluate which substrates have yielded successful results for your specific mushrooms and growing conditions. Learn from challenges and successes to refine your substrate selection for future cultivation endeavors.

Choosing the right substrate involves a careful balance of understanding your mushrooms' needs, considering environmental factors, and optimizing for accessibility and cost. By navigating the considerations outlined in this section, cultivators can make informed decisions that lay the foundation for a successful and bountiful mushroom cultivation experience.

# Preparing Substrates for Optimal Mushroom Growth

*Crafting the Canvas for Mycelial Prosperity*

Preparing substrates is a critical step in ensuring the success of your mushroom cultivation endeavor. In this section, we'll explore the step-by-step process of preparing substrates, creating an ideal environment for mycelial growth and setting the stage for a robust and fruitful harvest.

**Gathering Substrate Materials**

*Building the Foundation*

Begin the substrate preparation process by gathering the necessary materials. Explore the selection of substrates based on the requirements of your chosen mushrooms. Ensure the quality and cleanliness of materials to provide an optimal foundation for mycelial growth.

## Substrate Mixing and Composition

*Balancing the Recipe*

Dive into the art of substrate mixing, creating a balanced composition that caters to the nutritional needs of your mushrooms. Explore the ratios of different substrate materials, incorporating grains, sawdust, and additional nutrients to formulate a nutrient-rich blend.

## Sterilization Techniques

*Ensuring a Clean Canvas*

Sterilization is crucial to eliminate competing microorganisms and create a sterile environment for mycelial growth. Explore different sterilization techniques, such as pressure cooking or autoclaving, to ensure the complete elimination of contaminants.

## Pasteurization Methods

*Balancing Sterility and Nutrient Retention*

In certain cases, pasteurization may be preferred over sterilization to retain beneficial microorganisms. Explore pasteurization methods and when to use them based on your substrate composition and the requirements of your mushrooms.

## Adjusting pH Levels

*Fine-Tuning Acidity*

pH levels play a crucial role in mycelial growth. Learn techniques for adjusting and fine-tuning pH levels to create an environment that is conducive to the development of robust mycelium. Understand the importance of monitoring pH throughout the substrate preparation process.

## Moisture Content Management

*Nurturing the Right Hydration*

Balancing moisture content is essential for creating an environment that supports mycelial growth. Explore techniques for managing moisture levels during substrate preparation, ensuring that the substrate is neither too dry nor overly saturated.

## Inoculation and Seeding Substrates

*Planting the Seeds of Mycelium*

The inoculation phase marks the introduction of mushroom spores or mycelium to the substrate. Explore techniques for aseptic inoculation, ensuring the clean introduction of the fungal component. Learn about proper spacing and distribution to encourage even mycelial colonization.

## Incubation and Monitoring

*Nurturing Mycelial Prosperity*

After inoculation, provide the right conditions for mycelial colonization during the incubation phase. Explore the optimal temperature and humidity levels, and implement a monitoring system to track the progress of mycelial growth.

## Troubleshooting Substrate Issues

*Addressing Challenges with Finesse*

Substrate issues may arise during the preparation process. From contamination concerns to uneven mycelial growth, explore troubleshooting techniques to address challenges effectively. Learn how to identify and rectify issues to ensure the health and vitality of your substrate.

**Transition to Fruiting Conditions**

*Preparing for the Fruiting Stage*

As mycelium colonizes the substrate, prepare for the transition to fruiting conditions. Explore the adjustments needed in temperature, humidity, and light exposure to signal the onset of the fruiting stage and encourage the development of mushrooms.

By following these step-by-step guidelines for substrate preparation, cultivators can create an environment that nurtures optimal mycelial growth. Each phase, from gathering materials to transitioning to fruiting conditions, contributes to the successful cultivation of mushrooms, providing a rich and fertile canvas for the journey ahead.

# Chapter 3

# Growing Mushrooms: Step by Step

## Inoculation Techniques

*Planting the Seeds of Fungal Growth*

Inoculation is a pivotal step in the mushroom cultivation process, where spores or mycelium are introduced to the substrate. In this section, we'll explore various inoculation techniques, ensuring the clean and precise initiation of mycelial growth.

### Understanding Inoculation Basics

*The Gateway to Mycelial Colonization*

Begin by understanding the fundamentals of inoculation, the process that kick starts mycelial growth. Explore the importance of aseptic technique, maintaining a clean environment to prevent contamination and ensure a successful initiation of the fungal life cycle.

### Choosing Between Spores and Mycelium

*Spores vs. Mycelium: Selecting the Starting Point*

Delve into the decision-making process of choosing between spores and mycelium for inoculation. Understand the advantages and considerations of each option, evaluating which method aligns best with your cultivation goals and the requirements of your chosen mushrooms.

**Inoculation Tools and Equipment**

*Precision Instruments for Fungal Introduction*

Explore the variety of tools and equipment used in the inoculation process. From syringes and inoculation loops to flow hoods and glove boxes, understand the purpose of each instrument and how they contribute to maintaining aseptic conditions during inoculation.

**Spore Syringe Inoculation**

*9.1.4.1 Seeding Mycelium with Spores*

Learn the art of spore syringe inoculation, a common method for introducing spores to the substrate. Explore the steps involved in preparing and using a spore syringe, ensuring a controlled and clean distribution of spores across the substrate.

**Liquid Culture Inoculation**

*Harnessing the Power of Mycelial Liquid*

Dive into liquid culture inoculation, a technique that utilizes mycelial liquid to introduce fungal growth to the substrate. Explore the process of creating and utilizing liquid cultures, understanding how they offer a more concentrated and targeted approach to mycelial initiation.

**Agar-to-Substrate Inoculation**

*Transferring Mycelium to the Growing Medium*

Explore the agar-to-substrate inoculation method, where mycelium cultivated on agar plates is transferred to the substrate. Delve into the steps involved in this technique, understanding how it allows for the precise placement of mycelium on the growing medium.

**Inoculation Environment Setup**

*Establishing Aseptic Conditions*

Creating an aseptic environment is crucial for successful inoculation. Explore the setup of a clean and sterile space for inoculation, whether using a laminar flow hood, glove box, or other tools. Understand the measures to maintain cleanliness and prevent contamination during the inoculation process.

**Post-Inoculation Monitoring**

*Tracking the Journey of Mycelial Growth*

After inoculation, embark on the monitoring phase to track the progress of mycelial growth. Explore methods for observing and assessing colonization, ensuring that the substrate is developing a healthy and robust network of mycelium.

**Troubleshooting Inoculation Issues**

*1 Navigating Challenges with Precision*

Inoculation may encounter challenges, from contamination concerns to uneven mycelial growth. Explore troubleshooting techniques to address issues that may arise during and after the inoculation process, ensuring a smooth and successful initiation of mycelial colonization.

By mastering the art of inoculation and understanding the nuances of different techniques, cultivators can ensure a clean and effective start to the mycelial growth journey. Each method offers its unique advantages, allowing cultivators to choose the approach that aligns best with their cultivation goals and the specific requirements of their chosen mushrooms.

# Spore Syringes and Liquid Culture Methods

*Spore Syringes: Seeding Mycelial Growth*

Spore syringes are a common and accessible method for initiating mycelial growth in mushroom cultivation. Here's a comprehensive exploration of the spore syringe inoculation method:

**Creation of Spore Syringes**

Creating a spore syringe involves collecting spores from a mature mushroom's cap and depositing them into a sterile liquid solution. The solution, usually distilled water or a sterile saline solution, becomes the vehicle for distributing spores onto the substrate. The process requires meticulous attention to cleanliness, ensuring the syringe remains free of contaminants.

**Sterile Inoculation Process**

Inoculating with a spore syringe involves injecting the spore solution into the substrate, providing the spores with a fertile environment to germinate and develop into mycelium. Cultivators must adhere to strict aseptic techniques during this process to prevent contamination.

**Colonization Monitoring**

After inoculation, monitoring the substrate for mycelial colonization is crucial. Visual cues, such as the appearance of white mycelium spreading through the substrate, indicate successful spore germination and colonization. Maintaining optimal environmental conditions during this stage is essential for robust mycelial growth.

## Harvesting and Transfer

Once the substrate is fully colonized, the mycelium is ready for the next stage of the cultivation process. Harvesting may involve transferring the colonized substrate to a fruiting chamber, where the environmental conditions are adjusted to stimulate mushroom development.

*Liquid Culture Methods: Harnessing Mycelial Liquidity*

Liquid culture methods offer a more concentrated and targeted approach to inoculation by utilizing a liquid medium enriched with mycelium. Here's a comprehensive exploration of liquid culture methods:

## Creation of Liquid Culture

Creating a liquid culture involves introducing a small piece of mycelium from a culture or spore syringe into a liquid medium. This medium can consist of various nutrient-rich solutions, such as malt extract or potato dextrose broth. The mycelium grows and multiplies in the liquid, creating a potent inoculum.

## Advantages of Liquid Culture

Liquid cultures offer several advantages, including a higher concentration of mycelium compared to spore syringes. This method allows for more precise inoculation, as a smaller volume of liquid can deliver a substantial amount of mycelium to the substrate. Additionally, liquid cultures reduce the risk of introducing contaminants during the inoculation process.

## Inoculation with Liquid Culture

Inoculating with a liquid culture involves transferring a portion of the liquid mycelium to the substrate. This can be done using a syringe or another sterile instrument. The liquid culture method provides a controlled and targeted introduction of mycelium, promoting even colonization of the substrate.

## Colonization and Monitoring

Similar to spore syringe inoculation, the substrate is monitored for mycelial colonization after liquid culture inoculation. The mycelium should spread and colonize the substrate, forming a robust network. Maintaining optimal conditions during this phase is crucial for the success of the liquid culture method.

## Transition to Fruiting Conditions

Once the substrate is fully colonized, the transition to fruiting conditions is initiated. Adjustments in temperature, humidity, and light exposure signal to the mycelium that it's time to develop mushrooms. This transition marks the culmination of the liquid culture method, leading to the eventual harvest of mature mushrooms.

Both spore syringes and liquid culture methods offer effective means of initiating mycelial growth, each with its unique advantages. Choosing between them depends on factors such as accessibility, precision, and personal preference. By mastering these inoculation techniques, cultivators can set the stage for a successful and fruitful mushroom cultivation journey.

## Spore Syringes and Liquid Culture Methods

In mushroom cultivation, spore syringes and liquid culture methods serve as pivotal techniques for introducing fungal life to the substrate, initiating the mycelial growth process.

## Spore Syringes: Seeding Mycelial Growth

### Creation of Spore Syringes

Spore syringes are crafted by collecting spores from mature mushroom caps and suspending them in a sterile liquid solution. The solution, typically distilled water or a sterile saline solution, serves as the carrier for distributing spores evenly onto the substrate. The creation process necessitates a meticulous adherence to cleanliness to avoid any contamination.

### Sterile Inoculation Process

Inoculation with spore syringes involves injecting the spore solution directly into the substrate, offering the spores a nutrient-rich environment for germination and mycelial development. Maintaining a sterile environment during this process is paramount to prevent the introduction of unwanted contaminants.

### Colonization Monitoring

Post-inoculation, cultivators monitor the substrate for signs of mycelial colonization. The emergence of white mycelium spreading through the substrate indicates successful spore germination and colonization. Optimal environmental conditions are crucial at this stage to facilitate robust mycelial growth.

### Harvesting and Transfer

Once the substrate is fully colonized, the mycelium is ready for the next phase of cultivation. Harvesting involves transferring the colonized substrate to a designated fruiting chamber. In this environment, conditions are adjusted to stimulate mushroom development, leading to the eventual harvest.

## Liquid Culture Methods: Harnessing Mycelial Liquidity

### Creation of Liquid Culture

Liquid cultures involve introducing a small piece of mycelium from a culture or spore syringe into a nutrient-rich liquid medium. This medium can be a solution containing malt extract, potato dextrose broth, or other nutrients. The mycelium proliferates within the liquid, creating a concentrated and potent inoculum.

### Advantages of Liquid Culture

Liquid cultures offer advantages such as a higher mycelium concentration compared to spore syringes. This method provides a more precise and targeted inoculation, reducing the risk of introducing contaminants during the process. The liquid medium also allows for easy distribution and accurate measurement of the inoculum.

### Inoculation with Liquid Culture

Inoculating with liquid culture involves transferring a portion of the liquid mycelium to the substrate using a syringe or another sterile instrument. This method ensures a controlled and targeted introduction of mycelium, promoting even colonization of the substrate. The liquid culture approach is particularly useful for consistency in inoculation.

### Colonization and Monitoring

After liquid culture inoculation, the substrate is monitored for mycelial colonization. The mycelium should spread evenly through the substrate, forming a robust network. Maintaining optimal conditions during this phase is critical for the success of the liquid culture method.

**Transition to Fruiting Conditions**

Upon full colonization of the substrate, the transition to fruiting conditions is initiated. Adjustments in temperature, humidity, and light exposure signal to the mycelium that it's time to develop mushrooms. This transition marks the culmination of the liquid culture method, leading to the eventual harvest of mature mushrooms.

Mastering both spore syringes and liquid culture methods equips cultivators with versatile tools for initiating mycelial growth. The choice between these methods depends on factors such as precision, accessibility, and personal preference. By understanding and implementing these techniques effectively, cultivators can lay the foundation for a successful and fruitful mushroom cultivation journey.

# Incubation and Colonization

*Nurturing Mycelial Prosperity*

Incubation and colonization are crucial phases in mushroom cultivation, where the mycelium establishes a robust network within the substrate. In this section, we'll explore the art and science of fostering mycelial growth during the incubation and colonization stages.

**The Significance of Incubation**

*Creating the Ideal Growth Haven*

Incubation serves as the initial period after inoculation, during which mycelium establishes itself within the substrate. Explore the importance of providing optimal conditions, including temperature and humidity, to foster a healthy and vigorous mycelial network.

## Ideal Incubation Conditions

*Temperature and Humidity Harmony*

Delve into the ideal environmental conditions for incubation. Explore temperature ranges conducive to mycelial growth and the importance of maintaining adequate humidity levels. Learn how these factors influence the speed and strength of mycelial colonization.

## Monitoring Mycelial Progress

*Tracking the Network's Development*

Throughout incubation, vigilant monitoring is key. Learn how to observe the substrate for signs of mycelial growth, ensuring that the colonization process is progressing smoothly. Explore visual cues and indicators that signify a healthy and robust mycelial network.

## Troubleshooting Incubation Challenges

*Addressing Hurdles with Precision*

Incubation may encounter challenges, from uneven colonization to issues with environmental conditions. Explore troubleshooting techniques to address common incubation challenges, ensuring that the mycelial network develops uniformly and without hindrance.

## Transitioning to Colonization

*Preparing for the Substrate Takeover*

As incubation progresses, the mycelium establishes itself within the substrate, preparing for the colonization phase. Explore the visual cues that signal the end of incubation and the transition to full-scale colonization. Understand the factors that influence a seamless transition.

## Mycelial Colonization Dynamics

*The Fungal Conquest Unfolds*

Colonization marks the phase where mycelium proliferates, spreading and permeating the substrate. Dive into the dynamics of mycelial colonization, exploring how the network expands and consolidates its hold on the growing medium.

## Speeding Up or Slowing Down Colonization

*Adjusting the Mycelial Tempo*

Understand the factors that influence the speed of mycelial colonization. Explore techniques for accelerating colonization when conditions are optimal and slowing it down when necessary. Learn how to fine-tune the pace to achieve the desired results.

## Environmental Conditions for Colonization

*Providing the Colonizers with Ideal Habitat*

Explore the environmental conditions that support efficient mycelial colonization. From maintaining the right temperature and humidity to ensuring proper air exchange, understand how these factors contribute to a thriving mycelial network.

**Troubleshooting Colonization Challenges**

*Overcoming Roadblocks on the Mycelial Highway*

Colonization may face challenges such as contamination, uneven growth, or substrate issues. Explore troubleshooting strategies to address these challenges effectively, ensuring a healthy and robust mycelial colonization process.

By mastering the art of incubation and colonization, cultivators set the stage for a successful mushroom cultivation journey. The meticulous care and attention to environmental conditions during these phases contribute to the development of a strong and flourishing mycelial network, laying the foundation for a bountiful mushroom harvest.

# Providing Ideal Conditions for Mycelium Growth

Creating and maintaining ideal conditions for mycelium growth is essential for a successful mushroom cultivation journey. In this comprehensive guide, we'll explore the key factors and strategies to foster robust mycelial development.

**Temperature Optimization**

*Mycelium's Thermal Sweet Spot*

Mycelium thrives within specific temperature ranges, varying among mushroom species. Understand the temperature requirements for your chosen mushrooms during different growth stages. Maintain a stable and suitable temperature environment to promote vigorous mycelial growth.

## Humidity Management

*The Moisture Equation*

Achieving the right balance of humidity is critical for mycelium growth. Explore the optimal humidity levels required for your mushrooms, ensuring that the substrate remains adequately moist without becoming overly saturated. Implement strategies such as misting and humidity monitoring to maintain an ideal moisture balance.

## Air Exchange and Ventilation

*Breathing Room for Mycelium*

Providing fresh air exchange is vital for mycelium health. Implement a ventilation system to ensure a continuous supply of oxygen and the removal of carbon dioxide produced during mycelial respiration. Proper air circulation contributes to a healthy substrate and supports robust mycelium growth.

## Light Considerations

*Illuminating the Mycelial Realm*

While mycelium doesn't require light for growth, its presence can influence the initiation of fruiting. Understand the role of light in signaling developmental stages. Provide minimal light exposure during incubation and colonization, and prepare for increased light exposure when transitioning to the fruiting stage.

## Substrate Nutrition and Composition

*Crafting a Mycelium Feast*

The substrate serves as the primary source of nutrition for mycelium. Choose a nutrient-rich substrate and understand the nutritional needs of your specific mushrooms. Explore substrate composition, incorporating ingredients like grains, sawdust, and additional nutrients to support vigorous mycelial growth.

## pH Level Adjustment

*Balancing Acidity for Mycelial Harmony*

Maintaining the right pH level is crucial for mycelial growth. Regularly monitor the pH of the substrate and make adjustments if needed. Explore techniques for modifying pH levels using additives to create an environment where mycelium can thrive.

## Microclimate Customization

*Tailoring Conditions to Mycelial Preferences*

Different mushrooms may have specific microclimate preferences. Understand the unique requirements of your chosen mushrooms, including temperature, humidity, and air exchange. Customize the growing environment to match the ideal conditions for your specific mycelial species.

## Nutrient Timing and Supplementation

*Enhancing Mycelial Fitness*

Timing and supplementing nutrients during key growth stages can boost mycelial development. Explore strategies for nutrient supplementation, ensuring that the substrate remains enriched with essential elements throughout the cultivation process.

## Monitoring and Adjusting Conditions

*The Art of Mycelial Gardening*

Consistent monitoring of environmental conditions is essential. Regularly assess temperature, humidity, air exchange, and other factors to ensure they remain within the optimal range for mycelium growth. Make timely adjustments to address any deviations and provide a stable and supportive environment.

# Troubleshooting Mycelium-related Issues

*Navigating Challenges with Precision*

Mycelium may encounter issues such as contamination, uneven growth, or substrate concerns. Develop troubleshooting skills to identify and address challenges promptly, ensuring a healthy and flourishing mycelial environment.

By comprehensively addressing these factors, cultivators can create an environment that maximizes mycelium growth potential. The meticulous balance of temperature, humidity, air exchange, light, substrate nutrition, and other variables contributes to a robust and thriving mycelial network, setting the stage for a successful mushroom cultivation journey.

# Troubleshooting Common Issues During Colonization

*Navigating Mycelial Challenges*

Colonization is a critical phase in mushroom cultivation, and encountering issues during this stage is not uncommon. In this section, we'll explore common challenges that may arise during colonization and provide comprehensive troubleshooting strategies to ensure a healthy mycelial development.

## Uneven Colonization

*Addressing Patchy Growth*

Uneven colonization can occur for various reasons, such as uneven substrate distribution or inadequate inoculation. Explore techniques to promote even mycelial growth, including proper substrate mixing during preparation, ensuring consistent inoculation, and addressing any environmental factors contributing to patchy colonization.

## Contamination Concerns

*Identifying and Eliminating Contaminants*

Contamination is a common issue during colonization and can manifest as molds or bacteria competing with mycelium. Learn to identify signs of contamination early on, implement rigorous sterilization practices during substrate preparation, and explore methods for isolating and removing contaminated areas to salvage unaffected sections.

## Slow or Stalled Colonization

*Revitalizing a Lagging Mycelial Pace*

Slow or stalled colonization can be attributed to suboptimal environmental conditions, insufficient nutrients, or issues with the substrate. Explore strategies to troubleshoot and revitalize the mycelial pace, including adjustments to temperature and humidity, nutrient supplementation, and identifying and addressing substrate-related challenges.

## Fuzzy or Cottony Mycelium

*Understanding and Managing Fuzzy Growth*

Fuzzy or cottony mycelium can indicate high humidity levels or insufficient air exchange. Investigate the environmental conditions contributing to this type of growth, adjust humidity levels, and improve air circulation to encourage the development of healthier, rhizomorphic mycelium.

## Overly Wet or Dry Substrate

*Striking the Right Balance in Moisture*

Maintaining the correct moisture balance in the substrate is crucial. Address issues of overly wet or dry substrate by adjusting misting frequency, improving drainage, and fine-tuning humidity levels. Achieving the right moisture content promotes optimal mycelial growth.

## Abnormal Smells During Colonization

*Investigating and Remedying Odorous Issues*

Unusual odors during colonization may indicate bacterial contamination or other issues. Detect and identify abnormal smells, isolate contaminated areas, and take corrective actions such as adjusting substrate composition, enhancing sterilization methods, and ensuring proper air exchange.

## Discoloration of Mycelium

*Decoding Color Changes in Mycelium*

Changes in mycelial color can signal various issues, from natural metabolites to contamination. Learn to discern between normal pigmentation and signs of trouble. Address concerns such as green or black discoloration promptly by identifying the root cause and implementing corrective measures.

## Temperature Fluctuations

*Stabilizing Mycelium's Thermal Habitat*

Fluctuating temperatures can impact mycelial growth. Implement measures to stabilize temperature conditions, such as insulating the cultivation space, using temperature-controlling tools, and ensuring consistent environmental conditions throughout the colonization phase.

## Substrate Quality Issues

*Ensuring a Nourishing Substrate Base*

Issues with substrate quality can impede mycelial growth. Assess the composition of the substrate, ensure it meets the nutritional needs of your mushrooms, and consider adjusting formulations or incorporating supplements to address deficiencies.

## Light Exposure Concerns

*Mitigating Light-related Challenges*

While mycelium generally doesn't require light, prolonged exposure to light during colonization may impact certain mushroom species. Ensure that the substrate is adequately shielded from light during this phase to prevent any potential negative effects on mycelial development.

By systematically addressing these common issues during colonization and implementing effective troubleshooting strategies, cultivators can navigate challenges and ensure a healthy and robust mycelial development. Identifying and resolving issues promptly contributes to the overall success of the cultivation process, setting the stage for a fruitful mushroom harvest.

# Fruiting Conditions and Harvesting

*Cultivating the Harvest Bounty*

The fruiting stage is the culmination of the mushroom cultivation journey, where mycelium transforms into mature mushrooms. In this section, we'll explore the art and science of creating optimal fruiting conditions and executing a successful harvest.

## Initiating Fruiting Conditions

*Signaling the Transformation*

Transitioning from colonization to fruiting conditions involves a shift in environmental factors. Explore the key triggers for initiating the fruiting stage, including adjustments in temperature, humidity, and light exposure. Understand the signals that prompt mycelium to start the mushroom development process.

## Temperature and Humidity Adjustments

*Orchestrating the Fruiting Symphony*

Fine-tune temperature and humidity to create conditions conducive to mushroom development. Learn the optimal ranges for different mushrooms during the fruiting stage and implement adjustments to encourage the formation of primordia, the initial stages of mushroom growth.

## Light Requirements for Fruiting

*Illuminating the Fungal Stage*

While mycelium doesn't require light, mushrooms are phototropic and respond to light cues during the fruiting stage. Explore the role of light in triggering pinning and optimizing mushroom formation. Implement controlled light exposure to guide the developmental process.

## Fruiting Chamber Setup

*Crafting the Perfect Stage*

Design and set up a dedicated fruiting chamber to create an environment that supports mushroom growth. Explore considerations such as chamber size, ventilation, and humidity control. Implement techniques for optimizing the fruiting chamber to maximize the yield of mature and healthy mushrooms.

## Pinning and Primordia Formation

*Witnessing the Birth of Mushrooms*

Understand the process of pinning, where small mushroom primordia begin to form. Explore the environmental conditions and cues that trigger this developmental stage. Learn to recognize the signs of successful pinning and ensure the optimal conditions for primordia formation.

## Maturation and Mushroom Development

*Nurturing the Growth Process*

Once primordia form, mushrooms undergo maturation. Explore the stages of mushroom development, from the growth of the cap and stem to the expansion of the gills. Understand the environmental factors that contribute to healthy and robust mushroom maturation.

## Harvesting Techniques

*The Art of Mushroom Harvest*

Harvesting mushrooms requires precision and care to preserve both quantity and quality. Explore techniques for harvesting mature mushrooms, including the use of sterile tools, gentle handling, and proper timing. Learn how to encourage continuous flushes for extended harvesting periods.

## Post-Harvest Considerations

*Managing the Harvest Bounty*

After harvesting, ensure proper post-harvest care to maintain the quality and freshness of the mushrooms. Explore storage techniques, including refrigeration and drying, to prolong the shelf life of harvested mushrooms. Implement sanitation practices to reduce the risk of contamination post-harvest.

## Troubleshooting Fruiting Challenges

*Overcoming Hurdles in the Fruiting Stage*

Fruiting may encounter challenges, such as irregular pinning, stunted mushroom growth, or issues with environmental conditions. Explore troubleshooting strategies to address these challenges effectively, ensuring a successful fruiting stage and a bountiful harvest.

By understanding and implementing the principles of fruiting conditions and harvesting, cultivators can orchestrate the final act of the mushroom cultivation journey. The careful management of environmental factors, combined with precise harvesting techniques, contributes to the successful transformation of mycelium into a harvest bounty of mature and healthy mushrooms.

# Creating the Perfect Fruiting Environment

Creating the ideal fruiting environment is a pivotal aspect of successful mushroom cultivation. In this comprehensive guide, we'll explore the key elements and strategies to craft a perfect fruiting environment for maximizing mushroom yield.

## Fruiting Chamber Design

*Crafting a Mushroom Haven*

Designing an effective fruiting chamber is the foundation for creating the perfect environment for mushroom development. Explore considerations such as chamber size, ventilation, and lighting. Design a space that allows for optimal air exchange, humidity control, and light exposure to support the fruiting process.

## Temperature and Humidity Management

*Thermoregulation for Fruiting Success*

Fine-tune temperature and humidity levels to align with the specific requirements of your chosen mushrooms during the fruiting stage. Implement measures to maintain stable conditions, promoting the initiation and development of primordia. Understand the nuanced temperature and humidity preferences for various mushroom species.

## Light Exposure Optimization

*Illuminating the Path to Mushroom Growth*

Optimize light exposure to trigger pinning and guide the development of mushrooms. Understand the role of light in the fruiting process and implement controlled light cycles to simulate natural conditions. Ensure that mushrooms receive adequate but not excessive light during the fruiting stage.

## Air Exchange Strategies

*Breathing Life into the Fruiting Chamber*

Establish an effective air exchange system to provide mushrooms with fresh oxygen and remove carbon dioxide. Explore ventilation strategies to maintain optimal gas exchange within the fruiting chamber. Implement measures to prevent the buildup of stagnant air and encourage healthy mushroom development.

## Humidity Control Techniques

*Maintaining Moisture Balance*

Achieve precise humidity control within the fruiting chamber to create an environment that promotes mushroom growth. Implement misting systems, humidifiers, or other humidity-controlling tools to ensure consistent and adequate moisture levels. Monitor and adjust humidity to prevent over-saturation or dry conditions.

## Substrate Surface Conditions

*Creating a Favorable Substrate Microclimate*

Pay attention to the conditions at the substrate surface, where mushrooms initiate growth. Ensure a microclimate that encourages primordia formation by maintaining a slightly higher humidity level. Implement strategies such as misting or surface moisture management to create an optimal substrate surface for mushroom development.

**Fanning Techniques**

*Simulating a Natural Breeze*

Incorporate fanning techniques to simulate a natural breeze within the fruiting chamber. Understand the role of fanning in promoting air circulation, preventing the buildup of stale air, and supporting healthy mushroom development. Implement a fanning schedule that aligns with the specific needs of your mushrooms.

**Monitoring and Adjusting Conditions**

*Fine-Tuning for Optimal Growth*

Consistent monitoring of environmental conditions is essential during the fruiting stage. Regularly assess temperature, humidity, light exposure, and air exchange to ensure they remain within the optimal range for mushroom development. Make timely adjustments to create a stable and supportive fruiting environment.

**Avoiding Common Pitfalls**

*Navigating Challenges with Precision*

Anticipate and avoid common pitfalls that may arise during the fruiting stage, such as excessive moisture, insufficient air exchange, or inadequate light exposure. Implement proactive measures to address potential challenges and create a resilient fruiting environment.

By meticulously addressing these elements and implementing effective strategies, cultivators can create the perfect fruiting environment for their mushrooms. The careful orchestration of temperature, humidity, light, air exchange, and substrate conditions sets the stage for a prolific fruiting stage and a successful harvest.

# Harvesting Mushrooms at the Peak of Freshness

Harvesting mushrooms at the peak of freshness is a crucial step in the cultivation process to ensure optimal flavor, texture, and nutritional value. In this comprehensive guide, we'll explore the techniques and considerations for harvesting mushrooms with precision.

**Harvest Timing**

*Selecting the Perfect Moment*

Timing is essential in harvesting mushrooms for the best quality. Understand the optimal harvesting window for your specific mushroom species. Harvesting too early or too late can impact flavor and texture, so closely monitor the development of mushrooms and pick them at the peak of maturity.

**Proper Harvesting Tools**

*Gentle Touch with the Right Tools*

Select and use the appropriate harvesting tools to ensure a delicate and clean harvest. Consider tools such as scissors, shears, or a sharp knife. Avoid tearing or bruising the mushrooms during harvest, as this can impact their appearance and shelf life.

**Gentle Handling Techniques**

*Minimizing Trauma to the Harvest*

Handle mushrooms with care to minimize damage during the harvesting process. Avoid squeezing or compressing the mushrooms, as this can affect their texture and overall quality. Gently detach them from the substrate or growing medium to preserve their freshness.

## Complete Harvest Removal

*Ensuring a Clean Harvest*

Ensure the complete removal of harvested mushrooms from the growing medium. Leaving partial stems or remnants can attract contaminants and compromise the substrate's integrity. Conduct a thorough and clean harvest to maintain the health of the remaining mycelium.

## Harvesting Techniques for Different Species

*Tailoring Methods to Mushroom Varieties*

Different mushroom species may require specific harvesting techniques. Research and understand the unique characteristics of each species you are cultivating. Adjust your harvesting approach to accommodate variations in cap structure, stem thickness, and other features for an optimal harvest.

## Harvesting in Flushes

*Maximizing Yield through Flushes*

Many mushrooms produce multiple flushes or harvests. Learn to recognize the signs of subsequent flushes and implement strategies for harvesting in stages. By allowing some mushrooms to mature while others continue to develop, you can extend the harvesting period and maximize overall yield.

## Post-Harvest Handling

*Preserving Freshness Beyond Harvest*

Immediately after harvesting, handle mushrooms with care to maintain their freshness. Try to avoid exposing them to excessive heat or direct sunlight. Consider using breathable containers or baskets for transportation to prevent condensation and extend the post-harvest shelf life.

## Storage Considerations

*Optimizing Conditions for Longevity*

Implement proper storage techniques to preserve the quality of harvested mushrooms. Refrigerate them in a breathable container or a paper bag to maintain optimal humidity levels. Avoid storing mushrooms in airtight containers, as this can lead to excess moisture and spoilage.

## Utilizing Harvested Mushrooms

*Culinary Creativity Beyond Harvest*

Explore diverse culinary uses for harvested mushrooms. Incorporate them into a variety of dishes, from sautés and stir-fries to soups and salads. Experiment with different cooking methods to showcase the unique flavors and textures of freshly harvested mushrooms.

## Continuous Monitoring and Harvesting

*Harvesting as a Dynamic Process*

Continue monitoring the cultivation environment for signs of additional mushroom development. Harvest mushrooms as they reach maturity to maintain a continuous harvest cycle. Regularly assess and adjust harvesting strategies based on environmental conditions and the developmental stage of the mushrooms.

By implementing these harvesting techniques and considerations, cultivators can ensure that mushrooms are harvested at the peak of freshness, preserving their quality and nutritional value. A careful and attentive approach to harvesting contributes to the overall success of the mushroom cultivation journey.

# Chapter 4:

# Advanced Techniques and Troubleshooting

## Scaling Up Your Operation

*Elevating Cultivation to New Heights*

Scaling up your mushroom cultivation operation requires thoughtful planning, efficient processes, and a strategic approach. In this section, we'll explore the key considerations and strategies for expanding your cultivation endeavors successfully.

### Assessing Expansion Goals

*Defining Your Growth Objectives*

Clearly define your goals for scaling up the operation. Whether aiming for increased production volume, diversifying mushroom varieties, or entering new markets, a comprehensive understanding of your expansion objectives is crucial for guiding the scaling-up process.

### Infrastructure Planning

*Building the Foundations for Growth*

Evaluate and plan for the necessary infrastructure upgrades to accommodate increased cultivation capacity. Consider factors such as additional growing space, equipment, climate control systems, and sanitation facilities. Develop a blueprint that aligns with your expansion goals.

### Production Optimization

*Streamlining Processes for Efficiency*

Optimize cultivation processes to maximize efficiency and output. Identify areas of improvement in substrate preparation, inoculation, incubation, colonization, and fruiting. Streamline workflows to enhance productivity while maintaining the quality of mushroom cultivation.

## Resource Management

*Efficient Use of Resources*

Manage resources judiciously during the scaling-up process. Consider the procurement of raw materials, substrate components, and equipment. Evaluate energy consumption, water usage, and waste management to ensure sustainability and cost-effectiveness.

## Workforce Expansion and Training

*Cultivating a Skilled Team*

If expanding the workforce, focus on recruiting and training skilled personnel. Provide comprehensive training programs to ensure that team members understand and execute cultivation processes efficiently. Foster a culture of continuous learning to adapt to evolving cultivation practices.

## Quality Control Measures

*Upholding Standards in Growth*

Implement stringent quality control measures to maintain the high standards of your mushroom products. Regularly assess and refine processes to minimize variations and ensure consistency in mushroom quality. Establish protocols for monitoring and addressing any deviations in the production pipeline.

## Market Research and Diversification

*Navigating Markets for Growth*

Conduct thorough market research to identify potential niches and opportunities. Explore avenues for diversifying mushroom varieties and products to meet evolving consumer demands. Tailor your cultivation approach to align with market trends and preferences.

## Risk Management Strategies

*Anticipating and Mitigating Risks*

Identify potential risks associated with the expansion, ranging from environmental challenges to market fluctuations. Develop robust risk management strategies to mitigate and address potential issues. Ensure contingency plans are in place to navigate unforeseen challenges.

## Regulatory Compliance

*Adhering to Regulatory Standards*

Stay informed about local and regional regulations governing mushroom cultivation. Ensure that your expanded operation complies with safety, health, and environmental standards. Obtain necessary permits and certifications to operate within legal frameworks.

## Technological Integration

*Harnessing Technology for Efficiency*

Explore technological solutions to enhance efficiency and precision in cultivation processes. Consider the integration of automation, data analytics, and monitoring systems. Leverage technology to optimize resource utilization, improve decision-making, and maintain control over the cultivation environment.

**Continuous Evaluation and Adaptation**

*Iterative Growth Strategies*

Frequently assess the performance of your scaled-up operation. Collect data, solicit feedback from your team, and adapt your strategies accordingly. Embrace a culture of continuous improvement to refine cultivation practices and sustain long-term success.

By meticulously addressing these considerations, cultivators can scale up their mushroom cultivation operation successfully. The strategic planning, infrastructure development, and efficient processes contribute to a sustainable and thriving cultivation business capable of meeting growing market demands.

# Transitioning from Small Batches to Larger Productions

*Orchestrating Seamless Growth*

Moving from small batches to larger productions in mushroom cultivation requires a strategic approach to maintain efficiency and quality. In this section, we'll explore the key considerations and strategies for a smooth transition to larger-scale operations.

**Capacity Assessment**

*Understanding Growth Potential*

Conduct a comprehensive assessment of your current cultivation capacity and capabilities. Evaluate factors such as growing space, equipment, and resource availability. Determine the potential for scaling up while maintaining quality standards.

## Infrastructure Expansion

*Building a Foundation for Growth*

Plan and execute necessary infrastructure expansions to accommodate larger production volumes. Consider additional growing rooms, climate control systems, and processing facilities. Ensure that the expanded infrastructure aligns with your production goals and allows for seamless workflow.

## Equipment Upgrades

*Investing in Efficiency*

Upgrade cultivation equipment to handle larger volumes while maintaining efficiency. Consider automated or semi-automated systems for substrate preparation, inoculation, and harvesting. Invest in equipment that streamlines processes and reduces manual labor requirements.

## Streamlining Workflows

*Enhancing Process Efficiency*

Optimize cultivation workflows to streamline operations. Identify bottlenecks in small-batch processes and implement changes to enhance efficiency. Develop standardized procedures to maintain consistency as production scales up.

## Scaling Substrate Production

*Meeting the Demand for Substrate*

Assess and scale up substrate production to meet the increased demand. Ensure a reliable supply chain for substrate components and explore options for bulk purchasing. Implement quality control measures to maintain substrate consistency.

## Workforce Scaling

*Building a Skilled Team*

Scale up the workforce judiciously to match increased production needs. Focus on hiring and training skilled personnel who can adapt to larger-scale operations. Provide ongoing training to ensure that the team is proficient in handling the expanded cultivation processes.

## Quality Control in Larger Batches

*Upholding Quality Standards*

Implement stringent quality control measures to ensure the consistency and quality of larger batches. Regularly monitor and evaluate the production process, adjusting parameters as needed. Establish protocols for addressing deviations and maintaining high standards.

## Inventory Management

*Efficient Handling of Supplies*

Revise and optimize inventory management systems to accommodate larger production volumes. Implement real-time tracking systems for raw materials, substrate components, and harvested mushrooms. Ensure that supply chains are robust and can meet increased demand.

## Marketing and Distribution Strategies

*Navigating Larger Market Presence*

Revise marketing and distribution strategies to align with larger production capacities. Explore new markets and distribution channels to reach a broader audience. Consider partnerships with retailers, restaurants, and other stakeholders to expand your market reach.

## Risk Mitigation in Scaling Up

*Anticipating and Addressing Risks*

Identify and assess potential risks associated with larger-scale production, including environmental factors, market fluctuations, and supply chain vulnerabilities. Develop comprehensive risk mitigation strategies to address and navigate challenges that may arise during the scaling-up process.

## Continuous Monitoring and Adaptation

*Iterative Growth Strategies*

Continuously monitor the performance of the larger-scale production operation. Collect and analyze data to identify areas for improvement. Embrace a culture of adaptation and refinement, making iterative adjustments to processes, workflows, and strategies.

By systematically addressing these considerations, cultivators can transition from small batches to larger productions seamlessly. The strategic planning, infrastructure development, and optimization of processes contribute to a successful expansion that maintains the quality of cultivated mushrooms and meets growing market demands.

# Commercial Considerations for Mushroom Growers

*Navigating the Business Landscape*

Successfully navigating the commercial aspects of mushroom cultivation requires a blend of entrepreneurial acumen, market understanding, and operational efficiency. In this section, we'll explore key considerations for mushroom growers entering or expanding their presence in the commercial sphere.

## Market Research and Target Audience

*Understanding Market Dynamics*

Conduct thorough market research to understand current trends, consumer preferences, and potential competitors. Identify your target audience and tailor your cultivation approach to meet their demands. Stay informed about emerging market opportunities and adjust your strategies accordingly.

## Pricing Strategies

*Balancing Profitability and Accessibility*

Always Develop pricing strategies that balance profitability with market competitiveness. Consider factors such as production costs, quality standards, and perceived value. Implement dynamic pricing models that allow flexibility in response to market fluctuations and consumer demand.

## Marketing and Branding

*Cultivating a Distinctive Brand Identity*

Invest in marketing and branding to distinguish your mushroom products in the market. Develop a cohesive brand identity that communicates your values, quality standards, and unique selling points. Utilize online and offline channels to reach your target audience effectively.

## Distribution Channels

*Crafting an Efficient Distribution Network*

Explore and establish effective distribution channels for your mushroom products. Consider partnerships with local retailers, farmers' markets, restaurants, and grocery stores. Evaluate the feasibility of direct-to-consumer sales through online platforms. Build relationships with distributors to expand your market reach.

## Regulatory Compliance

*Navigating Compliance Standards*

Understand and comply with local, regional, and national regulations governing mushroom cultivation and distribution. Obtain necessary permits and certifications to operate legally. Stay informed about changes in regulatory standards and adjust your practices accordingly.

## Building Supplier Relationships

*Sourcing Quality Inputs*

Develop strong relationships with suppliers to ensure a reliable and consistent supply of raw materials, substrate components, and equipment. Negotiate favorable terms and explore opportunities for bulk purchasing to optimize costs. Maintain open communication to address any potential supply chain challenges.

## Financial Management

*Prudent Financial Planning*

Implement sound financial management practices to sustain and grow your mushroom cultivation business. Develop budgets, monitor expenses, and assess the return on investment for various aspects of your operation. Explore funding options and secure capital for expansion when needed.

## Scaling Operations Strategically

*Managing Growth Efficiently*

Strategically plan and execute the scaling of your cultivation operation to meet market demand. Consider the capacity of your infrastructure, workforce capabilities, and production efficiency. Monitor key performance indicators to ensure that scaling efforts align with financial and operational goals.

## Customer Feedback and Adaptation

*Responsive Business Evolution*

Solicit and analyze customer feedback to understand their preferences and satisfaction levels. Use this information to adapt and refine your products and services. Cultivate a customer-centric approach that builds loyalty and fosters a positive reputation in the market.

## Diversification Opportunities

*Exploring Additional Revenue Streams*

Explore opportunities for diversification within the mushroom cultivation business. Consider producing value-added products, such as dried mushrooms, extracts, or prepared meals. Evaluate collaborations or partnerships that can enhance your product offerings and market reach.

**Sustainability Practices**

*Embracing Eco-Friendly Initiatives*

Integrate sustainable practices into your cultivation and business operations. Consider eco-friendly packaging, energy-efficient systems, and waste reduction strategies. Communicate your commitment to sustainability, which can resonate positively with environmentally conscious consumers.

**Industry Networking and Collaboration**

*Building Alliances in the Industry*

Engage in industry networking and collaboration to stay informed about market trends, innovations, and opportunities. Attend conferences, join industry associations, and foster relationships with other growers, suppliers, and stakeholders. Collaborate on research and development initiatives to contribute to industry advancements.

By addressing these commercial considerations, mushroom growers can cultivate a successful and sustainable business. The integration of market insights, efficient operations, and strategic planning contributes to a thriving mushroom cultivation venture in the competitive commercial landscape.

# Common Challenges and Solutions in Mushroom Cultivation

*Navigating the Cultivation Journey*

Mushroom cultivation, while rewarding, comes with its share of challenges. In this section, we'll explore common obstacles faced by growers and provide effective solutions to overcome them.

## Contamination Issues

*Maintaining Sterility*

**Challenge:** Contamination by molds, bacteria, or competing fungi can jeopardize the cultivation process.

**Solution:** Implement rigorous sterilization practices during substrate preparation, inoculation, and throughout the entire cultivation cycle. Ensure a clean and dedicated workspace, use proper personal protective equipment, and regularly sanitize equipment and surfaces.

## Uneven Colonization

*Promoting Uniform Mycelial Growth*

**Challenge:** Uneven colonization can result in patchy growth, leading to suboptimal yields.

**Solution:** Address uneven colonization by thoroughly mixing substrate components, evenly distributing spores or inoculum, and maintaining consistent environmental conditions. Regularly monitor colonization progress and adjust factors like temperature and humidity to promote uniform mycelial growth.

## Temperature Fluctuations

*Stabilizing Thermal Conditions*

**Challenge:** Fluctuating temperatures can impact mycelial growth and mushroom development.

**Solution:** Stabilize temperature conditions within the ideal range for the specific mushroom species. Insulate the cultivation space, use temperature-controlling tools, and ensure consistent environmental conditions throughout the cultivation cycle.

## Slow or Stalled Colonization

*Revitalizing Mycelial Growth*

**Challenge:** Slow or stalled colonization can delay the cultivation process.

**Solution:** Identify and address factors contributing to slow colonization, such as suboptimal environmental conditions, insufficient nutrients, or substrate-related issues. Implement strategies to revitalize mycelial growth, including adjustments to temperature, humidity, and nutrient supplementation.

## Fruiting Challenges

*Encouraging Successful Fruiting*

**Challenge:** Issues during the fruiting stage, such as irregular pinning, stunted growth, or insufficient mushroom development, can impact yields.

**Solution:** Fine-tune environmental conditions, including temperature, humidity, and light exposure, to promote successful pinning and fruiting. Implement proper air exchange, maintain optimal substrate surface conditions, and address any issues promptly to ensure a healthy fruiting stage.

## Substrate Quality Issues

*Ensuring Nutrient-Rich Substrates*

**Challenge:** Substrate quality issues can impede mycelial growth and mushroom development.

**Solution:** Assess the composition of the substrate to ensure it meets the nutritional needs of the mushrooms. Adjust formulations or incorporate supplements to address deficiencies. Conduct thorough substrate preparation to create a nourishing base for optimal growth.

## Inoculation Challenges

*Achieving Successful Inoculation*

**Challenge:** Issues with inoculation can lead to uneven colonization or contamination.

**Solution:** Ensure aseptic conditions during inoculation. Use high-quality spore syringes or liquid cultures, and follow proper inoculation techniques. Minimize the risk of contamination by working in a clean environment and using sterile equipment.

## Harvesting Difficulties

*Precision in Harvesting*

**Challenge:** Harvesting requires precision to avoid damage and preserve quality.

**Solution:** Use appropriate harvesting tools, such as scissors or a sharp knife, to minimize damage. Harvest mushrooms at the peak of maturity, and handle them gently to prevent bruising. Thoroughly remove harvested mushrooms to maintain the health of the remaining mycelium.

## Environmental Factors

*Maintaining Ideal Growth Conditions*

**Challenge:** Fluctuations in environmental factors, such as humidity, light, and airflow, can impact cultivation.

**Solution:** Regularly monitor and adjust environmental conditions to maintain optimal growth parameters. Create a stable and controlled environment by utilizing tools such as humidifiers, ventilation systems, and lighting controls.

**Market Fluctuations**

*Adapting to Market Dynamics*

**Challenge:** Changes in market demand or conditions can impact the sale of cultivated mushrooms.

**Solution:** Stay informed about market trends and consumer preferences. Diversify product offerings, explore new markets, and establish flexible pricing strategies to adapt to market fluctuations.

By proactively addressing these common challenges and implementing effective solutions, mushroom cultivators can navigate the intricacies of the cultivation journey and achieve consistent success in their operations.

# Identifying and Addressing Potential Issues in Mushroom Cultivation

*Proactive Troubleshooting for Success*

In mushroom cultivation, recognizing and addressing potential issues promptly is crucial for maintaining a healthy and productive operation. In this section, we'll delve into key strategies for identifying and effectively addressing potential issues throughout the cultivation process.

## Regular Monitoring and Observation

*Vigilance for Early Detection*

**Strategy:** Establish a routine for regular monitoring and observation throughout the cultivation cycle. Actively inspect substrate conditions, mycelial growth, and the fruiting environment. Early detection allows for timely intervention before issues escalate.

## Diagnostic Tools and Testing

*Utilizing Technology for Precision*

**Strategy:** Incorporate diagnostic tools and testing methods into your cultivation practices. These may include pH meters, moisture sensors, or mycelium health assays. Implementing technology enhances precision in monitoring and provides data for informed decision-making.

## Environmental Parameter Control

*Fine-Tuning Growth Conditions*

**Strategy:** Maintain meticulous control over environmental parameters, including temperature, humidity, and light. Regularly calibrate and adjust systems to ensure consistency. Fluctuations in these conditions can signal potential issues, making precise control crucial for cultivation success.

## Record Keeping and Documentation

*Creating a Cultivation Journal*

**Strategy:** Maintain detailed records of each cultivation batch. Document substrate formulations, inoculation dates, environmental conditions, and any observed deviations. This information serves as a valuable reference for troubleshooting and refining cultivation processes.

## Collaborative Problem-Solving

*Engaging the Cultivation Community*

**Strategy:** Foster a collaborative approach to troubleshooting by engaging with the cultivation community. Participate in forums, attend conferences, and seek advice from experienced growers. Sharing insights and experiences can offer alternative perspectives and solutions to common challenges.

## Proactive Contamination Prevention

*Prioritizing Aseptic Practices*

**Strategy:** Prioritize aseptic practices to prevent contamination issues. Implement rigorous sterilization methods during substrate preparation, inoculation, and other critical stages. Regularly clean and sanitize equipment, surfaces, and the cultivation environment.

## Rapid Response to Deviations

*Swift Action for Issue Resolution*

**Strategy:** Develop a protocol for swift response to deviations from the expected cultivation process. If issues arise, investigate promptly, identify the root cause, and implement corrective measures. Timely intervention minimizes the impact on the overall cultivation cycle.

## Continuous Learning and Adaptation

*Embracing a Growth Mindset*

**Strategy:** Cultivate a continuous learning mindset within your cultivation team. Encourage ongoing education, attend workshops, and stay informed about advancements in mushroom cultivation. The ability to adapt and apply new knowledge enhances your troubleshooting capabilities.

**Integrated Pest Management**

*Proactive Pest Control Strategies*

**Strategy:** Implement integrated pest management (IPM) strategies to proactively address pest issues. Regularly inspect growing areas for signs of pests and deploy preventative measures, such as beneficial organisms or natural repellents, to minimize the risk of infestations.

**Flexible Cultivation Plans**

*Adapting Plans to Circumstances*

**Strategy:** Maintain flexibility in your cultivation plans to adapt to unforeseen circumstances. If issues arise, be prepared to adjust schedules, environmental conditions, or even the choice of mushroom species to optimize outcomes and mitigate challenges.

By incorporating these proactive troubleshooting strategies into your mushroom cultivation practices, you can enhance your ability to identify, address, and prevent potential issues. A vigilant and adaptable approach contributes to a resilient and successful cultivation operation.

# Disease Prevention and Management in Mushroom Cultivation

*Safeguarding Your Crop*

Disease prevention and management are paramount in maintaining a healthy and productive mushroom cultivation operation. In this section, we'll explore strategies for preventing and effectively managing diseases that can affect mushrooms.

## Strive for Aseptic Conditions

*Foundation of Disease Prevention*

**Strategy:** Maintain strict aseptic conditions throughout the cultivation process. Implement rigorous sterilization practices during substrate preparation, inoculation, and other critical stages. Minimizing the introduction of contaminants is foundational to disease prevention.

## Quarantine Measures

*Preventing Contaminant Spread*

**Strategy:** Establish a quarantine area for incoming materials, substrates, or contaminated cultures. This helps prevent the spread of potential contaminants to the main cultivation environment. Inspect and test materials before introducing them to the production area.

## Healthy Spore and Culture Sources

*Ensuring Pathogen-Free Inoculum*

**Strategy:** Source spores and cultures from reputable and reliable suppliers. Choose healthy, disease-free strains to minimize the risk of introducing pathogens. Regularly test and verify the quality of spore syringes or liquid cultures to ensure they are free from contaminants.

## Monitoring Environmental Conditions

*Tailoring Conditions to Prevent Disease*

**Strategy:** Regularly monitor and maintain optimal environmental conditions for mushroom growth. Ensure proper ventilation, humidity levels, and temperature control. Deviations from these conditions can create an environment conducive to the development of diseases.

## Early Detection and Isolation

*Swift Response to Disease Signs*

**Strategy:** Train cultivation staff to recognize early signs of diseases, including abnormal growth patterns, discoloration, or unusual odors. Implement a protocol for swift isolation of affected batches to prevent the spread of pathogens to healthy mushrooms.

## Proper Waste Disposal

*Minimizing Disease Reservoirs*

**Strategy:** Establish proper waste disposal practices to minimize the accumulation of potential disease reservoirs. Promptly remove spent substrate and other organic materials. Consider composting or disposing of waste in a manner that reduces the risk of disease transmission.

## Biosecurity Measures

*Implementing Strict Biosecurity Protocols*

**Strategy:** Develop and enforce biosecurity protocols to control access to cultivation areas. Require personnel to adhere to hygiene practices, including changing into clean clothing, using designated footwear, and washing hands thoroughly. Limit external factors that could introduce contaminants.

## Pathogen-Specific Strategies

*Tailoring Approaches to Specific Diseases*

**Strategy:** Familiarize yourself with common pathogens affecting mushrooms and tailor prevention and management strategies accordingly. This may include specific treatments, fungicides, or environmental adjustments to deter the growth and spread of particular pathogens.

## Genetic Resistance

*Selecting Resistant Mushroom Varieties*

**Strategy:** When feasible, select mushroom varieties known for genetic resistance to specific diseases. Breeding or selecting strains with inherent resistance can be an effective long-term strategy for disease prevention.

## Continuous Education and Research

*Staying Informed for Proactive Management*

**Strategy:** Stay abreast of current research on mushroom diseases and cultivation practices. Attend workshops, conferences, and engage with the cultivation community to remain informed about emerging diseases and innovative management strategies.

## Isolation Chambers for Troubleshooting

*Controlled Environments for Diagnosis*

**Strategy:** Designate isolation chambers for troubleshooting and disease diagnosis. Isolating affected batches allows for closer inspection and diagnosis without risking the spread of pathogens to healthy areas.

**Collaboration with Experts**

*Consulting Plant Pathologists*

**Strategy:** Establish relationships with plant pathologists or experts in fungal diseases. Collaborate with professionals who can provide insights into disease identification, prevention, and management tailored to mushroom cultivation.

By implementing these strategies, mushroom cultivators can significantly reduce the risk of diseases affecting their crops. A proactive and well-informed approach to disease prevention and management is essential for ensuring the long-term health and productivity of a mushroom cultivation operation.

# Conclusion

## Celebrating Your Mushroom Harvest

*Culminating the Cultivation Journey*

Celebrating your mushroom harvest is a joyous occasion that marks the culmination of hard work, dedication, and a successful cultivation journey. In this section, we'll explore ways to celebrate and make the most of the fruits of your labor.

### Harvest Festival

*Community Celebration*

**Celebration Idea:** Organize a harvest festival to celebrate with your community. Invite friends, family, and fellow growers to join in the festivities. Create a vibrant atmosphere with music, food, and activities centered around mushrooms.

### Culinary Delights

*Gourmet Mushroom Feast*

**Celebration Idea:** Showcase the versatility of your freshly harvested mushrooms by preparing a gourmet feast. Experiment with various culinary creations, from sautés and soups to mushroom-infused dishes. Host a dinner party to share the delectable flavors with others.

### Mushroom Tasting Event

*Tasting Flight of Varieties*

**Celebration Idea:** Arrange a mushroom tasting event to introduce different varieties to enthusiasts. Provide samples of your harvest and offer insights into the unique flavors and textures of each mushroom species. Pair the tasting with wine or other complementary beverages.

## Educational Workshops

*Sharing Cultivation Knowledge*

**Celebration Idea:** Give back to the community by hosting educational workshops on mushroom cultivation. Share your experiences, insights, and tips with aspiring growers. Encourage hands-on participation to inspire others to embark on their own cultivation journeys.

## Mushroom Art and Crafts

*Creative Expression*

**Celebration Idea:** Engage in mushroom-themed art and crafts to celebrate the harvest. Create mushroom-inspired paintings, sculptures, or crafts that reflect the beauty and diversity of your cultivated varieties. Display the artwork at your cultivation site or share it with the community.

## Farmers' Market Presence

*Showcasing Your Harvest*

**Celebration Idea:** Set up a booth at a local farmers' market to showcase and sell your freshly harvested mushrooms. Interact with customers, share your cultivation journey, and offer tips on mushroom preparation. Engaging with the community adds a celebratory dimension to the market presence.

## Mushroom Tasting Menu at Restaurants

*Collaboration with Local Eateries*

**Celebration Idea:** Collaborate with local restaurants to create a special mushroom tasting menu. Provide them with your freshly harvested mushrooms, and work together to develop unique dishes that highlight the flavors and textures of the mushrooms. This collaboration can bring your harvest to a wider audience.

## Community Mushroom Forays

*Exploring Wild Mushrooms*

**Celebration Idea:** Organize community mushroom forays to explore the natural environment and discover wild mushrooms. Engage a mycologist to guide the foray and share insights into local mushroom varieties. It's a celebration of the broader world of fungi beyond cultivated varieties.

## Mushroom Photography Contest

*Capturing Fungal Beauty*

**Celebration Idea:** Host a mushroom photography contest, encouraging participants to capture the beauty of mushrooms in creative and artistic ways. Display the winning entries at a celebratory event or showcase them on your cultivation website or social media platforms.

## Mushroom-Themed Merchandise

*Commemorative Merchandise*

**Celebration Idea:** Create mushroom-themed merchandise, such as T-shirts, hats, or mugs, to commemorate your harvest. These items can serve as keepsakes for your team and can be offered to customers or participants in your celebration events.

By incorporating these celebration ideas into your mushroom cultivation journey, you not only acknowledge the success of your harvest but also share the joy with your community. Whether through culinary experiences, educational outreach, or creative expressions, celebrating your mushroom harvest enhances the sense of accomplishment and connection within the cultivation community.

# Reflecting on Your Journey as a Mushroom Grower

*Contemplating Growth and Success*

Reflecting on your journey as a mushroom grower is an essential part of personal and professional development. In this section, we'll explore the significance of introspection and provide prompts to help you contemplate your growth, challenges, and successes as a mushroom cultivator.

## Embracing Growth and Learning

*Personal and Professional Development*

**Reflection Prompt:** Consider the knowledge and skills you've acquired throughout your journey as a mushroom grower. How have you personally and professionally grown during this process? Identify specific areas of improvement and celebrate the milestones you've achieved.

## Navigating Challenges

*Overcoming Obstacles*

**Reflection Prompt:** Recall the challenges you encountered during cultivation. How did you approach and overcome these obstacles?

Reflect on the lessons learned from setbacks and how they contributed to your resilience as a mushroom grower.

## Celebrating Successes

*Acknowledging Achievements*

**Reflection Prompt:** Take a moment to acknowledge and celebrate your successes as a mushroom cultivator. Whether it's a bountiful harvest, successful troubleshooting, or positive community engagement, recognize the milestones that have brought a sense of accomplishment to your journey.

## Building Community Connections

*Connecting with Fellow Growers*

**Reflection Prompt:** Consider the relationships you've built within the cultivation community. How have these connections enriched your journey? Reflect on the mutual support, shared knowledge, and collaborative experiences that have contributed to a sense of belonging in the mushroom-growing community.

## Sustainable Practices

*Incorporating Environmental Stewardship*

**Reflection Prompt:** Contemplate the sustainability practices you've integrated into your cultivation methods. How have you prioritized environmental stewardship in your operation? Reflect on the impact of these practices and explore additional ways to enhance the sustainability of your mushroom cultivation.

## Inspiring Others

*Sharing Knowledge and Passion*

**Reflection Prompt:** Reflect on your role as an inspiration to others interested in mushroom cultivation. How have you shared your knowledge, passion, and experiences with aspiring growers? Consider the impact of your efforts in encouraging others to embark on their own mushroom-growing journeys.

## Future Aspirations

*Setting Goals and Aspirations*

**Reflection Prompt:** Contemplate your future aspirations as a mushroom grower. What goals do you envision for your cultivation operation? How do you see yourself contributing to the broader cultivation community in the coming months and years?

## Cultivating a Growth Mindset

*Embracing a Learning Mentality*

**Reflection Prompt:** Assess your mindset towards learning and growth. How have you embraced a growth mindset in the face of challenges and new experiences? Reflect on the importance of continuous learning and adaptation in the dynamic field of mushroom cultivation.

## Balancing Passion and Practicality

*Nurturing Your Love for Mushrooms*

**Reflection Prompt:** Reflect on the balance between your passion for mushrooms and the practical aspects of cultivation. How have you maintained enthusiasm while addressing the day-to-day responsibilities of running a cultivation operation? Consider strategies to nurture both your love for mushrooms and the practical demands of cultivation.

**Expressing Gratitude**

*Recognizing Support and Opportunities*

**Reflection Prompt:** Express gratitude for the support, opportunities, and resources that have contributed to your journey. Reflect on the individuals, organizations, or circumstances that have played a significant role in your growth as a mushroom grower.

Take time to reflect on these prompts, journal your thoughts, and embrace the insights gained from contemplating your journey as a mushroom grower. The reflective process fosters a deeper understanding of your experiences, values, and aspirations, shaping the ongoing narrative of your cultivation adventure.

# Appendix:

**Resources for Mushroom Growers**

*Appendix A: Recommended Reading*

1. **"The Mushroom Cultivator" by Paul Stamets and J.S. Chilton**

   - An in-depth guide covering various cultivation techniques and the biology of mushrooms.

2. **"Growing Gourmet and Medicinal Mushrooms" by Paul Stamets**

   - A comprehensive resource on growing a wide range of gourmet and medicinal mushrooms.

3. **"Mycelium Running: How Mushrooms Can Help Save the World" by Paul Stamets**

   - Explores the ecological roles of mushrooms and their potential impact on environmental sustainability.

4. **"Radical Mycology: A Treatise on Seeing and Working with Fungi" by Peter McCoy**

   - An exploration of mycology from a holistic and regenerative perspective.

5. **"Organic Mushroom Farming and Mycoremediation" by Tradd Cotter**

   - Combines mushroom cultivation techniques with mycoremediation applications.

*Appendix B: Online Communities*

1.  **Shroomery (shroomery.org)**

    - A popular online forum covering various aspects of
      mushroom cultivation, with a focus on both
      beginners and experienced growers.

2.  **Reddit's Mushroom Growing Community
    (reddit.com/r/MushroomGrowers)**

    - An active community where growers share their
      experiences, ask questions, and provide advice.

3.  **Mycotopia (mycotopia.net)**

    - A community dedicated to mycology, offering
      resources on cultivation, identification, and other
      mushroom-related topics.

*Appendix C: Educational Courses and Workshops*

1.  **Fungi Perfecti (fungi.com)**

    - Founded by Paul Stamets, Fungi Perfecti offers
      online courses covering various aspects of
      mushroom cultivation and mycology.

2.  **North American Mycological Association (NAMA)
    Workshops (namyco.org)**

    - NAMA organizes workshops and forays to promote
      the study and appreciation of wild mushrooms.

3.  **Mushroom Cultivation and Identification Courses (local
    mycological societies)**

- Check with local mycological societies or agricultural extension offices for in-person courses and workshops in your area.

*Appendix D: Suppliers and Equipment*

1. **Field & Forest Products (fieldforest.net)**

   - A supplier offering a variety of mushroom cultivation supplies, including spawn, substrates, and tools.

2. **Mycelium Emporium (myceliumemporium.com)**

   - A source for spores, cultures, and cultivation supplies, catering to both beginners and experienced growers.

3. **Mushbox (mushbox.co)**

   - Provides mushroom cultivation kits and supplies, suitable for beginners and those looking for convenience.

4. **Shiitake Mushroom Log Kits (multiple suppliers)**

   - Various suppliers offer shiitake mushroom log kits, providing a simple way to grow mushrooms at home.

*Appendix E: Regulatory Considerations*

1. **United States Department of Agriculture (USDA)**

   - Check USDA regulations and guidelines for the cultivation and sale of mushrooms.

2. **Food and Drug Administration (FDA)**

- Be aware of FDA regulations related to the processing and sale of mushroom products.

3. **Local Health Departments and Agriculture Agencies**

- Consult local health departments and agricultural agencies for specific regulations and permits related to mushroom cultivation in your region.

Please note that the resources mentioned in this appendix are based on information available up to my last knowledge update in January 2022, and it's advisable to check for the latest information and updates from these sources.